Remember, It's OK

Loss of a Partner

Remember, It's OK

Loss of a Partner

MARINA L. REED
MARIAN GRACE BOYD

NEXT CHAPTER
PRESS

Remember, It's OK: Loss of a Partner

Copyright © 2020 by Marina L. Reed and Marian Grace Boyd

ISBN: 978-1-989517-03-1

All rights reserved.

Editor: Allister Thompson

Book Designer: Jamie Arts

Published in Stratford, Canada, by Next Chapter Press, an imprint of Blue Moon Publishers.

Printed and bound in Canada.

The authors are gratified that you chose this book to be with you during your grief. Please consider leaving a review wherever you bought the book, or tell others about *Remember, It's OK: Loss of a Partner*. We can all help and support each other in the grief journey.

Table of Contents

OTHER BOOKS IN THE REMEMBER, IT'S OK SERIES

Loss of a Parent

Loss for Teens

OTHER NEXT CHAPTER PRESS BOOKS ABOUT GRIEF AND LOSS

THE WISH I KNEW GRIEF COLLECTION

Conscious Grief & Loss Guide

Conscious Grief & Loss Guide Workbook

Gentle Quotes on Grief & Loss

Grief & Loss Guided Journal

To all those who have lost their partner,
the love of their life

FOREWORD

Although we all unconsciously know death is always present, lurking, on the periphery, biding its time to enter our lives, we are content to keep it out of our awareness. Nothing can prepare us for the loss of one who is deeply loved.

Remember, It's OK is a testament to the power of love and the innate healing potential within each one of us. I loved the time and space made to honour grief, the searing honesty, and the ascent back to life and a reforged self. This book provides us with a way forward and allows us to move through all the tumultuous emotions grief throws our way. The authors use six colours as the road map forward, one that calls to our emotional selves, from Red through to Pale Blue. They show there is light at the end of the journey.

Remember, It's OK, doesn't allow us to short change the all-encompassing reach of death and loss. We begin to understand that it is not only the loss of our loved one, but also the loss of a life and the self that no longer exist. We are uplifted by the words of the support person, sparse, compassionate, understanding, containing seeds of hope.

Remember, It's OK, is a gift, a gem, for all who have lost a loved one. It is an enlightening guide for friends, colleagues, family members, therapists, and those in the helping professions, allowing them entry into a world that can only be known by those who have been unwilling travellers in this terrain of loss. After reading this beautifully written book, it will no longer be possible or even desirable, to dismiss, shrink, and relegate grief into a small, manageable package.

Having worked as a therapist for twenty years, grief has made many trips through my office door. I wish *Remember, It's OK*, would have been available for all of us: my clients, their friends, family, colleagues, and myself. This book is an inspirational demonstration of allowing, welcoming, and being supportive of whatever presents itself during the grief process. It is a beautiful dance between a courageous griever, the wise and talented companion, and the love lost. There are no timelines, no right or wrong, simply a person and deep honouring.

A process that doesn't limit itself to survival but creates opportunities for profound healing, growth, and transformation.

I hope you find this book as beautiful, heart-wrenching, and ultimately triumphant as I did.

Sincerely,

Karen Harrington,
Psychotherapist
(B.A., M.A. Psychology/Grief Counselling)

ABOUT THIS BOOK, REMEMBER, IT'S OK.

Navigating the waters of grief for those who have lost a loved one, and those who want to help a grieving loved one.

Remember, It's OK is an experiential book. You will live this book, not just read it.

Remember, It's OK is a series of books dealing with specific types of losses. This first book deals with the loss of a partner, a spouse, a significant other. It has been written in the point of view of a woman but is equally viable and pertinent to loss that a man suffers. If you are a man reading this book, we humbly ask that you substitute 'he' for 'she' and make this your own personal journey. The same is true whether your partner was a man or a woman. This book is for anyone who has lost the love of their life. Period.

Even though some of the moments refer to interactions with children the couple may have had together, not everyone has children. Please feel free to insert step-children into those moments, as well as godchildren, nieces or nephews, or dear friends. Whatever is right for you.

We also want to mention that grief does not know religion, and we invite you to heal regardless of your religious affiliation. Special events and celebrations can be difficult when you have lost someone. Since we could not include special occasions from each religion, we have included moments around Christmas because it is widely celebrated and recognized. Again, we humbly ask that you substitute your religious holiday in its place; the feelings will still be similar. Thank you so much.

Please recognize that this book supports the loss of your loved one, no matter how they passed away. This book is for you, the one left behind.

Grief is not a linear process. The 'stages of grief' were initially designed by Kübler-Ross in order to support palliative patients. It was never designed for people who have experienced loss. Rather than moving from one stage to another, grief is a journey that cycles back and forth, in and out, as you find your way home. Please use this book to support how you feel, regardless of how much time has passed between now and when you experienced your loss. Explore the different colour sections and use the Moments that work for you. Go from colour to colour as you see fit, what works for you each day. You may find that you read all of Red two or three times and even come back to it when you are at the end of the book, and that's OK. It is your journey.

Colours have universal themes that have resonated throughout history. The colour choices were instinctual for us from the beginning:

RED: survival, urgency

ORANGE: beginning to find self, immediacy

YELLOW: coming back to self, growing awareness

GREEN: learning to balance self, learning

TURQUOISE: what path am I on now, increased awareness and curiosity

PALE BLUE: clarity of new path, beginning to move forward, increased openness

We have left blank pages after the Yellow and Pale Blue Moments for you to insert your own personal story, drawings, reminders, photos, struggles, achievements, joys, and sorrows. It will be something for you to learn from and reflect upon as you continue on your grief journey. Please don't leave them blank. Start another journal if you feel inspired and need more pages.

RESEARCH BEHIND THE BOOK

The authors drew upon countless discussions, interviews, and sessions with people who have suffered loss over the years to arrive at reoccurring issues and themes. These are the Moments that you find in *Remember, It's OK*.

ACKNOWLEDGEMENTS

We would like to acknowledge all the people who have shared their stories with us in order for others to be supported in their grief journey. We would like to thank our friends, our family, and our children for helping us bring this very special book into reality. The cowriters are indebted to each other for the organic process that inspired them to create *Remember, It's OK*, and the deep dedication to the project. Thank you to Lorraine Bordiuk, an aura-soma practitioner, for her consultation in colour therapy. And to Allister Thompson for editing our manuscript in the masterful way that he does. And finally, to all readers searching for the path back to themselves, we hope that we have enriched and enabled your journey.

Red
Moments

Nothing is the same. No warm home to come back to, no hugs, no comfort. I can't think of one thing that is easy or pleasant in my life right now. Every thing is hard, and there truly is no language for this continual anguish. Others tire of grief quickly, but grief never seems to tire of me. People ask, "How are you?" but they don't want to know. They don't want to see or hear about it. They have no understanding and no real compassion." "It will get better." "Time heals all wounds." "You're strong, you will be fine." "One day at a time, things will improve." "You'll find someone new." "This too will pass." You kidding me? Seriously? Fuck and fuck again. No way does this pass or get better. I just get better at pretending and never answering the question. In fact, I tell people to not ask me how I am. Just don't ask. But when something goes wrong, something happens and I need to run to my love for advice or comfort or help, that is an extended horror. That's where I would find answers or humour and lots of hugs and maybe a carefully poured tumbler of Scotch. No one else knew me like my sweetheart, no one else really cared about problems at work or in my heart. Now where do I go? Call my kids? They listen, but I can tell they would rather not, so I stop calling about issues, I talk about their lives, not mine. I try my friends, but friends are good for shopping and lunching. They have their own lives too and really don't want to be part of my crisis. Not any more. My dog sees my face and goes into the other room; even he wants no part. Sometimes I will wander in a bush, hug trees, and scream silently in abject agony. The tree holds me. I feel better for the release, but I still come home to walls and furniture. I really don't know why I have to be here alone. All the lessons and things I need to learn — CRAP. "Things happen for a reason." Right. Sure! I want my love back, or I want to be there too. No one really cares about me. Not really. So I have to figure it out for myself, for better or worse. Seems like a whole lot of 'worse.'

Nothing is good enough right now — there is no answer, there is no place, there is no person, there is no conversation, there is no escape that is good enough to reduce the pain of your grief and loss. Instead, all of these things have become irritants and are heightening your loss. Your loved one would have known what to do. Your loved one knew you. Your loved one learned what you needed. Your loved one was good enough. He was your love, your soul mate, your life — nothing can compare to that. Nothing.

There will be small things that will help soften your pain for a moment. These conversations are little moments; it's OK. Keep reading. It's OK.

I can't escape pain. Especially not the kind designed by grief. The ache that spreads across my chest, a desire to hide behind my eyes rather than seeing the images that lurk in front, a frenzy to push back thoughts creeping to the forefront of my mind, all become too much to bear. I can just turn and walk the other way, pretending they don't exist. But they do. And they will be heard. So as I enter this new road, the grief pain settles into my muscle tissue, in places already weak and ailing. And the longer I walk that road of distraction, the grief is weaving deeply around that tissue, curling into nerve endings. It will only allow me to sleep a few hours at a time and then clamp down and shock me into awakeness, awareness. I become fatigued and weary. The physical pain now overrides everything else. I can't ignore it any longer. No amount of physio or pills or even exercise will help. It is demanding that I look at my sadness, my pain. Grief is needy. But once I begin to give it the attention it craves, look into the shadows, pull apart the interwoven stitching, the physical discomfort diminishes bit by bit. Does the muscle tissue ever heal completely once assaulted by this intruder?

Your body is feeling the pain of grief. Think of all the things that have changed for your body: smells, sounds, touch, sight, and taste — have all been hit by a tornado. Think about how intricately your thoughts and feelings are intertwined with your physical body. Your body is not only expressing your grief; it is experiencing loss itself. How it expresses it will be important for you to notice. You may need to see your MD if your blood pressure rises or lowers too much; if your appetite leaves and you are too weak; if you can't sleep or oversleep to the point where it is interfering with your functioning. Your body will eventually be able to calm and find healing again, but for now, practical things like making sure you drink enough water, hot, soaking baths, sticking to a rhythm of eating and sleeping as much as you can will help your body.

All right. I'll try.

Blank Page Suggestion:
Colour the page in your favourite colour or colours.

Red Moment

it's raining outside
puddles pool around my feet
where snowdrifts should be
collecting
i can't avoid the puddles
my socks are wet
and cold
mist drapes itself
around cedars
and water droplets
clinging to evergreens
are pulled down
into
the puddles
one might be bottomless
but my feet
slosh in murky
mud
you are not here
to pull me
out
the mist has
enveloped me
i sit in a cold
puddle
and evaporate

All I can do is sit and listen. Are there others who would sit in that puddle with you? I do hope so. If not, know you will not evaporate.

I keep feeling like I'm going to throw up, and I haven't eaten anything for days. And when I try to sleep, the voices in my head are just screaming. Sometimes I don't even know what they're saying. But I can't get away. I can't get away from myself. I feel so uncomfortable in my body, like it isn't mine, like I don't want to be in it. I'm caught in between something. I've put a TV into my bedroom, but I can't be in there alone. My daughter took time off from university to come home. She lies on the bed beside me. There are sitcoms playing on the TV, but I don't really know what's going on. Nothing makes sense. All I want to do is scream, or cry, or just, I don't know, that's the problem. I don't know. I'm numb and hypersensitive at the same time. Food won't go down my throat. If I close my eyes and drift off even for a minute, I wake up in a panic. For a moment, the tiniest of moments, I think I've had this awful, awful nightmare, and I'm so glad I have finally woken up. I turn and look for my other half, and it all washes over me as I see my daughter asleep beside me, the TV in the room, and I want to throw up again. Because it's not a nightmare in my sleep; my life has become the nightmare, and I can't wake up.

I'm sitting in silence.

Your whole being, including your body, is in chaos. Grief changes who we are for a time — voices in our head, sleepless, numb, hypersensitive, not able to eat, not able to be alone, panic, a sick feeling... not who you usually are. So you don't know yourself, and that is really scary.

Every part of your being is in turmoil.

Right now, it's about finding ways to help reduce the intensity — like your daughter with you in bed: such a good plan for you right now. A TV in your room — good for you. Drinking a cup of tea. The body likes clear fluids right now. They seem like such little things, but it is the little things right now that will help make it through the chaos.

Your words bring me gratitude, unexpected gratitude.

Sometimes grief feels endless. E n d l e s s. I can't stand being alone and how haunted all the rooms feel. I can't stand being an outcast because no one likes the discomfort and pain I bring into a room. I can't stand pretending to be happy. I can't stand pretending that I want to be alive, because I don't. I see no point to anything. I can't stand not having my love to talk to and help me. I can't stand shopping alone. I can't stand eating alone. I can't stand trying to make sense of things by myself, because nothing makes sense. I can't stand feeling like a burden to my children. They don't want me to call all the time, even though it brings comfort to talk to them. It's too much for them. They want all things to be OK, and things are not OK. I'm not sure if they will ever be OK again. I can't stand being half. I can't stand not feeling like I'll ever be whole again. I can't stand people being cruel. I can't stand my children not really knowing how very raw I am, and that a simple tone makes me feel unloved and unworthy. His death has left me fragile and alone...I can't stand where I stand. My god, I just can't stand any of it.

Sometimes, in early grief, you will feel hopeless, and grief feels endless. Where is the hope that you will be able to survive this hard, dark place? Sometimes you will need to allow someone else, someone who has been through the valley of death and has survived, to be your hope-holder.

I can't think of anyone.

Why don't you write the word 'hope' on a piece of paper and drop it inside a clear glass or vase. Let that hold your hope for now.

Never would have thought of that. I'll try that. Thanks.

Blank Page Suggestion:
Draw just a simple line drawing (or cut and paste from a magazine or
the Internet) a container with the word 'hope' inside. It's your reminder.

There's this weird feeling, like a big part of me is not there any more.
And I'm staring into a hole.
A very black hole.

Tell me more about the hole.

Blank Page Suggestion:
What does your hole look like? Can you draw it or write a circle of words to describe it?

YOU PROMISED ME YOU WOULD NEVER LEAVE ME.
YOU PROMISED WE WOULD DIE TOGETHER.
YOU PROMISED IN WORDS YOU WROTE IN CARDS TO ME.
YOU PROMISED WITH WORDS YOU SPOKE TO ME.
YOU PROMISED.
YOU PROMISED.
You promised.
You promised.
You promised.
You promised.

He promised. He would have done anything he could to keep that promise.

How do I believe anyone again?

In this moment, it's unimaginable. Not now. Now, it's OK to be angry and disappointed, and disillusioned, and all the feelings you have. I'm fine with all your feelings.
They will soften — they will.

I feel like I am an observer of my life now.
I'm not part of it any more.
I'm outside looking in.
I feel that no one will ever really see me or know me again.
I am on my own now.
Isolated.
Alone.

You are seen.

That makes me smile.

Blank Page Suggestion:
Tell me about something you love or just draw some colours on the page in different shapes.

31

He always said he would never hurt me. Never leave me. I believed him and let myself settle into him and this magical life. I gave up my backup plan. He abandoned me like everyone else. He has hurt me more than I ever thought possible. Nothing else compares to this grief and loss and pain. I want to scream every moment. I now have nothing. I put everything into his basket. I am lost without him. Disillusioned. I want no part of this life, this game, this disaster. I want out. I can trust no one ever again. I am a dishcloth balled up in the corner of the sink.

You have been deeply, deeply hurt. I know. You trusted. Your tender, limp heart has been deeply hurt — all the more so because you learned how to trust. What now?

Exactly. What now.

I don't know what your grief journey will look like. For now, that's all right.

Blank Page Suggestion:
Draw where you are sitting or standing right now, or write words
about it.

Red Moment

I hate all these photos. I hate them. I can't bear to see the photos framed and on the walls, on the tables, on the mantle. Photographs of my love holding me, kissing me, the way he would look at me. I want to take them all and throw them out. Like he threw me out. And then I want to take them all into my bed and squeeze them until he comes back to life. We come back to life. I can't look at them any more. I'm taking them all down. Putting them in the back of a closet. I won't throw them out just yet. Can't do it. Want to, but can't. Now I'll look at holes in the wall reflecting the holes in my heart, in my soul. I don't want his photographs anymore; he abandoned me.

In the middle of your life together, in the middle of making all the photos of life and love and adventures, he left. There were things to do that were planned, and he left. He left. He didn't want to, but he had no choice...and it feels exactly like abandonment. I get it.

Right now, the photos cause too much pain and remind you that he left. It's fine to take them down, to put them away for a while. Please don't throw them out. Not yet. Not like this. You may want to look at holes for a bit, or you may want to put up some paintings that comfort you. But this is about you and what you can do with your space to reduce the pain just a bit.

Do you need help to put the photographs away? Who can you call?

Blank Page Suggestion:
List the photographs that need to be put away for a while. Get it
out of your head; it will help.

35

His bathrobe still hangs on the hook on the back of our bathroom door. His razor sits in its holder on the bathroom counter, beside his toothbrush. His jeans are draped over the back of the chair in our bedroom, his socks balled up on the floor. I hate how he leaves his socks all over the floor. But I won't pick them up. He put them there, for god's sake. How can I ever move them? His hats perch on their hooks. His sunglasses sit beside his car keys. His shoes are scattered about. His leather jacket is on its hanger in the hall closet, waiting for his form to fill it out. His collared shirts hang on their hangers in our bedroom closet. Everything is folded in the correct drawer. It's all there, waiting for him. My life is surreal. I'm stuck between two panes of glass and can't move. Can't move myself or anything else.

Could you use a hot drink right now?

Yes, surreal. That's a good word for it. Surreal...you are surrounded by what was real in an unreal world. It's OK to be still in this place. Be still. If you aren't ready to move yourself or any object, yours or his, then don't. You will find a time when you feel ready to move, when you feel ready to move things. Right now, for you, it's a time to be still. And that is fine.

A time to be still. I will take a breath; I am trying to take a breath and hear your words.

Blank Page Suggestion:
Make a list of things left by your love that you see every day. Slowly cross things off this list as you are able to deal with them.

The slightest issue gives me a headache and makes my stomach hurt. I seem to have no filter, no stamina, no stomach for errors. Any little problem can throw me off the bus, and I land in a crumpled little heap. My husband was my balance. I didn't really know that when he was alive. I knew he was a great support, but I didn't realize how much I depended on him to weigh things with me and help me filter. And he'd wrap me in those big arms and everything would just disappear and be all right. Because it didn't really matter what it was, it would be good because we had each other and looked after things together. Now, it's only me. I have to deal with everything and everyone, and that is exhausting. My eye starts to twitch and my stomach starts to hurt. It's hard to eat when the stomach is churning. I always thought I was quite resilient and a bit tough, able to handle things. I'd always be the one to take on phone companies or hydro, or anyone else giving us a hard time. My husband would hand the issue over to me: "You deal with these people better than me honey, you show 'em" — and I would. But now, I don't want to 'show' anyone. It's like my chutzpah died when my husband died. And things seem bigger — my stupid cell phone won't dial and hold a signal, it constantly disconnects, passwords don't seem to work, I have to renegotiate the mortgage and seem to have forgotten how, the dishwasher is not draining again, I can't figure out the hydro bill...oh my god. It wasn't meant to be done alone. I hate it, I hate it all. I miss my honey. I just want him back. I just want him back.

I know you do.

Grief is exhausting you. Everything takes so much more effort. Your head aches, your stomach hurts, low interest and energy, and, yes, no chutzpah. Taking care of your body will at least help you to have a bit of energy. Remember to connect with your doctor and practitioners (chiropractor, massage therapists, natural healers, etc.) that can support you. Remember to eat, drink water, get some sunlight. You are also experiencing some foggy thinking — it's harder to have the clarity that you had before. Everything is seen through the lens of grief.

Oh, if he would just come back.

Tiny little white pills. Lorazepam. They were left on the counter for me. I wanted to take them all and anything I could find in the bathroom. But I only took one. I needed to sleep. Thing is, it made things worse. I kept dreaming through this fog, and it was hard to open my eyes and get up, and I heard a knocking at the door and I knew it was him, and I needed to get to the door or he would disappear again. But I was paralyzed. Groggy. Terrified. I wouldn't get to the door in time. I couldn't help him. I couldn't save him. I should have done more, tried something. Anything. It's all my fault. When I finally woke up I flushed all the remaining pills down the toilet. More exhausted than usual. A cloak of heaviness all over me. Maybe I could have done more. Maybe if I had just listened more carefully, been more observant. Oh my god, there are so many maybes and what-ifs pounding around in my head. Was it all my fault? Maybe he would still be here if I had just…I don't know. But I must have missed something.

The next day, a friend brought over some marijuana cookies. "They will just mellow you out, help you sleep," she said. I said thank you and put them in the almost empty fridge, remembering the dream and the little white pills. They stared at me each time I opened the door. So did the bottle of wine. Maybe if I drank enough, had a few cookies, I could just pass out on the couch. Stop these thoughts in my head. I'm soooo tired, and I can't stand the pain any more. The doubt. I stand with the fridge door open. I don't know what to do.

Help me.

Your whole being wants it to end, to be released from this unimaginable pain. What do you think the pills or cookies or alcohol will do for you?

I don't know. Maybe sometimes I want to go and be with him. I can't imagine being here without him. Odd to say that out loud.

These thoughts surprise you? It may surprise you to know that these are thoughts and longings that grieving people have when someone very dear has died. And your friends don't like seeing you this way, and they don't know what to do other than offer a quick fix: pills, alcohol, cookies, etc. They have good intentions, to be sure, but they don't understand grief. They can't. They don't sit in your chair. They are only looking from afar. Your friends care about you, and that is meaningful. But it is OK to say thanks, but no thanks.

You know, it wasn't your fault.

No, I don't know that. I really don't. If I had listened more. Pressed the doctors harder. Asked more questions. Not been at work so much. Not been away. Oh god, maybe it was all my fault. Maybe he wanted to leave. Oh, that is such a hard thought.

Our "if only" thoughts circle around us and trying, trying desperately to find the reason. We look at blaming ourselves, our loved one, the doctors, someone! There has to be something that will make sense of this thing that has happened that has turned your world upside down. "If only" I could figure that out!! "If only! Then..."
What do you think your "then" is?

Then he'd still be here.

You would have done anything and changed everything to have kept him here. That's the depth of your love. And of your pain.

It's nearing the end of November. My sweetheart and I would begin to put up decorations now. We had so much fun. He'd be on the ladder, and I'd hand him ornaments and wreaths, joking and laughing the whole time. He was always cracking jokes. We'd work on lights outside together and think about the Christmas tree we'd put up soon. And all the holiday movies would come out of their box in the closet for the season. Our house was so festive and welcoming. It doesn't feel so festive this year. I don't like ladders. In fact, I don't think I'll even get the box of ornaments and wreaths out of their boxes. And a Christmas tree is out of the question. Instead of laughter and hugs and tears of gratitude and joy, I find it hard to get out of the chair in the living room. All the holiday movies are filled with love and kisses and reunions. Not death. It's like I've been sucked out of my own body, and instead there is this shell that resembles me, but it's very heavy and reluctant to move and devoid of lighter emotions. I can't bear to watch one happy holiday movie, so I stick to sports, where there's noise and movement and a lot of anger, which fits me well. Or just the silence. Christmas, once filled with noise and laughter and largeness, has become very small and tiny and quiet. Fragile. Broken. As if at one single moment all the ornaments on a Christmas tree fell to the floor and smashed into a million pieces. The tree is bare, the floor dangerous to walk on without shoes. So, I stay in my chair.

I'm glad you have that chair.

Remember to be kind to yourself...guess that is becoming a theme, isn't it? Finding ways to take a break from the intensity, a "back door" when you make plans, safe people to be with, giving yourself permission to say 'no' to invitations that feel like too much, having a candle lit beside you whenever you sit in your chair, maybe a nice fragrance, or perhaps go away over the holiday season...these are the kinds of things that will help you survive.

It will be hard, but you already know that. It's OK to hibernate in your chair. For now.

What if I can't get out? What if I can't afford to go anywhere or have anyone I can go to?

Remember that grief takes a lot of energy. Right now, you may not have the energy to move very far from your chair. As you are kind to yourself, as you listen to yourself, you will begin to find a wee bit of energy coming back.

Blank Page Suggestion:
Make a list of some plans that won't cost much or take a lot of energy
but could be good for you.

I couldn't alter his fate. Can I do anything about mine? My children's? Or are we just puppets in a cruel experiment? It feels like death is all around me. Like all there is — is death.

Big loss sure brings hard questions. Questions you didn't have to think about before. And a new kind of relationship with death that you never had to be aware of. Feels so much more unpredictable, doesn't it?

That's what scares me. I'm afraid everyone I love is going to die now.

I know. It does feel like that right now. Your face has been smacked up against death, and that's all you can see. Slowly, you will begin to move your face back, and you will be able to take your eyes off death. You're OK.

I'm OK. I'm OK.

It's November 11, Remembrance Day.
I'm traumatized.

Can you tell me about that?

So much death. So much loss. Everyone's screams of loss and pain are mingling with mine.

...like being flooded with a deluge of grief and loss.
    I hadn't thought about it like that before. I get it.
You aren't ready to remember yet.
    How do you stop the flood? This won't be the year for you to 'do' November 11th; step back and shut away from it as much as you can. Being kind to yourself means guarding yourself against floods.
    Take a deep breath.
    A long, deep breath.

I'm trying. I really am.

I know you are.

If all we have is the moment, the today, then how do we begin to separate ourselves into pieces free of grief? How does it all work if there is nothing before or after? Only grief seems to be everywhere.

Right now, it does seem to be everywhere...like a veil or a blanket settling down over everything. Making it hard to see or breathe. Is that kind of what it feels like?

That's exactly it. Will I be able to keep breathing?

Yes, you will keep breathing. Sometimes you will remind yourself not to hold your breath and tell yourself, "just breathe." It will become a familiar voice in your head: "just breathe." It will help slow you down, find the ground, and be still in moments where you feel overwhelmed. Just breathe. Just breathe.

My daughter thought it might be good to watch a movie. I can't stand hearing any voice, no news, no music, because all the lyrics speak about what I have lost, so no music. I don't really want people around, but I don't want to be alone. So, fine, a movie. She puts on an animated movie about a dragon. And I think this will be OK. After all, it's a kid's movie, it's animated, not real life. Should be fine. Distract my mind from the constant pain, from the thoughts that circle around and around each other, darker and darker. So, we have a glass of wine, or at least I try to sip at it, and we put the movie on. And I like the dragon, and the small boy, and my mind begins to soften, and I watch and listen to something other than ghosts. My daughter laughs in parts and is enjoying her wine. And then a small moment happens in the movie, and I panic. I think the dragon is going to die. I say this to my daughter, who has seen the movie, and she says, "No. Mom, it's OK, it really is OK," but my mind has gone, it's left the quiet space and I'm terrified. I'm not sure why, but I'm shaking and now I'm standing behind the couch and I'm screaming and crying, "Turn it off, TURN IT OFF, TURN IT OFF," and I'm hysterical. I can see me from the outside, but I can't do a thing about it. I can see I've scared my daughter. She looks panicked as she fumbles to find the remote and turn off the TV. "There, it's off, it's off, Mom," and she's yelling at me, which makes me even worse. Now I'm clutching the back of the couch, shaking, crying, and I don't know what to do. She just sits there. And we wait. I eventually stop crying and bring myself to sit down beside her. I take her hand, and we just sit there, in the silence sitting in the middle of chaotic screams and fears and loss and longing. Am I going crazy?

No. You aren't going crazy. This is what grief can feel like. Grief makes us more fragile and vulnerable — loud sounds, voices, music lyrics...all feel like they are attacking our small and fragile self. We desperately try to protect ourselves. And when it happens, in spite of all our efforts, we are desperate to find balance again — and we may yell, or scream, or hide, or turn the music off...all good things for us to do for ourselves right now. When we are so deeply wounded, the only thing we can think about is survival and protecting our very being.

No. You aren't going crazy.

Good. Scares the shit out of me, though.

I know.

When my love died, I stood on the threshold of the doorway he left through. I can't follow him, because I still have a body, but it feels like being caught between both worlds. I realize there is much more to our life than the physical and what meets the eye. It's hard to compartmentalize it all, like we humans do with everything, as it is so huge. So, I wander, feel aimless, and forget to do things my body needs: food, washing. There seems little reason for anything. Having a bath or a shower just looks like a huge pointless effort. Let's face it, who knows when I'll be crossing that threshold myself? But I am still in the body. A friend of mine came over to make me soup one day. I don't know what day. I don't know days any more. I didn't feel like chatting, at all; I was listening for sounds of my love. I was a bit lost in the silence, but there was a comfort in that as well. When he was alive, there weren't enough minutes in the day to do everything...now I sit for hours, I just sit. Sit. My friend made squash soup, gentle but nourishing. I sipped at a cup she gave me. She talked about her kids, the weather; it was like background noise to me. Then she said my name a few times until I paid attention. "You should have a shower," she said. "Why?" I asked. "Because, my dear, you don't smell very good." "Oh." "And I'll take those clothes you've been wearing for three days and wash them." "OK." So she ran a shower for me and supervised me, making sure I actually did use shampoo, like a child. It felt better after, like washing some of the pain down the drain, and the fog in my brain. It was good to put on clean clothes, like coming back over that threshold. She brought me another bowl of soup, fed the dog (I couldn't remember if I'd done that in the last few days), kissed my cheek, turned on the TV for me, and left. She left. S H E   L E F T. There was too much noise and movement in the TV. I turned it off and just sat and sipped the soup, just sat and sipped.

Your friend knew exactly what to do — help you survive. She took care of the very basics, and that's all you needed. That's all. That's all. Sit and survive. She did this for you, and you found out it helped. I'm glad.

I stumble into the forest behind my house. I am tired. I haven't slept in days. Things are blurry. I find myself moving farther and farther into the darkness of the underbrush. Branches and leaves pushing into my body. I have left the path. I want to disappear. I want to leave. I want to go where my love has gone. I don't want to be here without that person, I don't want to be here alone. I trip and find myself on the ground. I stay there, hoping the earth will open and swallow me. Take me away from this agony, this oppressive fog. I pound my fists into the earth, making dents and divots. I can't pound hard enough. I pull myself up and stagger forward, swatting away branches harder and faster. They swing back, hitting me in the face, in my head. I feel blood trickling down my face, mingling with my tears. I am numb. I am enraged. I am exhausted. I don't want to be here. "Where are you? Where are you?" I begin to scream. I fold my arms around a tree in front of me and continue screaming. Blood-curdling screams that rivet through my body like electric staples from a gun. I clutch into the bark, digging it under my nails, pulling myself into the tree, and I scream louder and louder until I can't hear myself any more, I can just feel the sound in my body and against the bark as it shudders with the vibration. And as I scream, I feel tears and sweat pour out of my body until I have nothing left, and I slide down into a crumpled cracked heap onto the ground.

I am sitting silently. Tears on my cheeks hearing your pain.

Blank Page Suggestion:
Draw or cut and paste a tree on the blank page. If you have no trees nearby to hold that can absorb your pain, use your blank page tree and a pillow. It helps to release emotion.

I was a lovely wool sweater, intricately woven, warm, and cozy. But when my love died, a small piece of wool became unstitched. As days passed, the small piece of wool became longer and longer, making it difficult to put on. Soon it was pulled out and snapped off, to get it out of the way, and the knitting stitches started to unweave. The sweater slowly began to unfurl until soon there were only armpits and sleeves. Not much of a sweater any more. The piece of wool ended there. There is another piece that could be attached to a new ball of wool, and the sweater could be reknit. It will never be the same again. Colours will all be off, and the tightness of stitch will be different. For now the sweater sits, taken apart, in the sewing box. Whether or not it will come to life again is a question not yet answered.

Someday, when you are ready, you will find those knitting needles. You have kept the yarn and put it in a safe place for the right day.
  It will come to life again. It will.

I hope so, I really do.

Orange
Moments

I had a dream last night that has really unsettled me. I dreamed that my son died of a heart attack, and I had a panic attack that woke me up, I couldn't breathe. I have not been able to go to work today; my blood pressure is through the roof, and I still have a terrible headache…and I was doing so much better. I had a dream that my husband would die a month before he did — is my son going to die too? The dreams were slightly different in nature, but it has deeply upset me. I feel like I am being punished for something, and I am finding it very hard to live on this planet without my love. I feel so insecure and impatient. Now, I am rattled. Not sure how to recover. Do you have some thoughts for me?

Those are hard dreams. They can spin you into panic and fear and feel so real. Death has become real in a way it never was before; your dreams are trying, so desperately trying, to find ways to make sense of death, to predict it, to protect against it, to see it coming… your dreams have also been impacted by his loss. In your waking hours, you are hypervigilant right now; and in your sleep, you are also hypervigilant. Knowing that this is a normal and helpful part of your grief journey might help you as you find ways to comfort yourself through the panic and fear. Keeping a light on in your room, playing soft music as you sleep, a sweet aroma in your room (those oil diffusers are great) can be ways to help you feel comforted both as you sleep and when you awaken after a dream.

Your dreams will change and soften as your grief responses begin to soften. For now, knowing that they may come, you can find ways to soften their strength.

It does help to know this. Makes me feel less at the mercy of grief. I like the idea of the oil diffuser. Maybe a lavender scent.

Perfect. And it's safe and doesn't need a lot of attention.

Ok, I'll try that. Thanks.

I was only given five days off. Five days to deal with the loss of my love, of my life. Then back to work. What choice do I have? I'm numb as I get into the car and drive, boxes of Kleenex on the passenger seat because I just start crying for no apparent reason, and then I can't see where I'm going. There are balled-up tissues all over the floor on the passenger side. I can't listen to the news on the radio because every story makes me think of what I've lost, what I don't have; every disaster is mine. I can't listen to music because every song has a memory of my lost love, every love song makes my heart crack all over again. I didn't know I had that many tears inside me; they just keep pouring out. My eyes are red and puffy each day as I go through work motions like a zombie, trapped inside this bubble of agony.

One day, I'm driving home and it is February and a storm whips up. All of a sudden, snow is everywhere. I can't see, and I begin to panic. It would be at this moment I would call my love, and he would calm me down and I would know it would be OK. But today, I realize with a jolt that spins through my veins like liquid ice, there is no one at the other end of the phone. There is no one there when I get home. In fact, no one would even know if I ended up in the ditch and froze there. No one is waiting for me. No one cares. I am alone. I am alone. I am alone. I can't see for the tears and the snow. I pull over and fall asleep. When I wake up it is dark. I'm cold. The snow is still blowing. I pull back onto the highway, more numb than when I began. Just wanting to step into that dark hole that seems to pull at me. I am alone. I am alone.

Can you tell me a bit about this hole now?

I don't know. It sits there, getting bigger and bigger. Sometimes it feels like the only option I have is to step forward and into it. And there will be peace there. Sometimes it feels like there is this tiny little space I have to walk on, and other than that, it is all black, a black hole. It sits there, getting bigger and bigger. Sometimes it feels like a thin path of aloneness, of nothing, of no one. Maybe I should just step into the hole.

What do you think would happen if you stepped into the hole?

It would all stop. It would all go away. I'd be free of this eternal agony. This constant crying.

What do you think is keeping your feet grounded on the thin space around the hole?

I don't know. I don't know. It's solid. I can feel it. But the hole has such pull.

In your picture of the hole and the thin space you stand on, can you turn away from the hole for a moment and tell me what you see?

It's hard to turn, I feel off-balance. It's such a thin, solid space. One foot at a time. OK, I don't see a hole. I see a tree.

The thin space becomes a path, a meadow, a field, a place with a tree. It's a thin space right now around the hole. It feels like such a pull because there really isn't much other space to be in. As you take one little step at a time, in the thin space, you will find that the thin space begins to spread and get wider for you. That your steps won't be so off-balance. And the hole, yes, it will still be there, but you will begin to find more trees, and the hole will have less pull.

OK. So when I feel that pull, that pull into the dark hole, I can turn myself around. Right?

Yes. You will be able to do that because you will begin to see that the thin space is growing. You will begin to feel a pull toward this growing space. Begin to see what is on this side of the hole.
I am so glad you made it home all right. You must have been exhausted by the time you got home.

Yes. Still am.

Do something kind for yourself.

Blank Page Suggestion:
What does your hole look like, and the space behind?

I am not meaning to complain here, but I guess I need to tell you this. It was suggested that I connect with someone to support me, someone who had been through a loss, someone who could help me. So, when a woman was presented to me, I tried. I emailed a few times and texted. But when I asked her a question about how it could get better, really, her answer was that basically that it was good what I had before, but now I need to look to a new life. And that just put me into tears, because I don't want a new life. I don't even want this one now; I'm just being responsible, as always. And so much of my life with my love remains as it is, because things need to finish. They're just not finished, you know? Anyway, so now I've lost faith in talking with other people, supports, because I think they will all say the same thing, and that just won't help me. It pushes me farther back. And obviously she has found a new life and is settled with that. I can't imagine that. I can cope and have tricks to do that, but little else. I feel dried and brittle, like a maple leaf in autumn just waiting to crack into a million pieces.

Sadly, you have discovered that not everyone that has experienced loss will be a safe support for you. A safe person will not feel they need to fix your feelings or make you feel better by telling you what to do. A safe person will listen and learn from you. The circle of safe people may be very small right now. Thank you for letting me be part of your circle. You will know when you meet someone else who will be a safe support for you. I have confidence in you.

Grief.
It is burning coals in your eye sockets
And
muscles on the rack
that circle your head.
It is knives through
the heart
through the top of your head
between your toes.
It is nausea
And
Dis   belief.
It is a questioning of self-
Worth.
It is lonely
It is the most
Unpalatable
Gruesome
All-encompassing
Experience.
I wish it
on
no
One.

No one. Totally agree.

How do I live with him gone? How do I live knowing that if I'd helped him more with his meds, he might still be here? Or if I had listened to his complaints, I would have been able to call someone sooner. Or if I hadn't gone to work that day, I would have been around to prevent the disaster. Or if I hadn't been so upset about the dishwasher, he wouldn't have been stressed. Or if we had gone to visit the kids that week. Or if I'd taken him for a checkup…How can I live with all these 'or ifs' and 'what ifs'? They are suffocating me. I feel like the life is being squeezed out of me. I'm haunted. What if it was my fault?

If only you knew what was about to happen. If only. When something awful happens, we want to find a reason and something or someone to blame. There will be times you will blame him. There are times, like now, when you blame yourself. You may find yourself playing and replaying events of his death, trying to think of something that could have been done to change what happened! Yes, you will replay the event. It's so hard to not have answers. Would anything that you might have done differently change the outcome?

Maybe. Maybe if I had been more sensitive to how he was feeling, and we went back to the doctor. But I still wouldn't have known to ask for certain tests to be done. I just wouldn't have. That all came out after. Then I knew what I, or we, should have done. But on my own, before he died? No. Nothing. You're right. There was nothing I could have done. It was going to happen. I'm glad I loved him as much as I did. At least I have that.

Yes. You do have that. You loved very deeply. That is clear.

Blank Page Suggestion:
List your 'what ifs.' Get them out of your head. Let the page hold them for you instead.

Orange Moment

What if I forget him?
I don't want to forget him.
I hope I don't forget him.
I hope he doesn't forget me.

You won't.
He won't.
Truly.

I'm sad today. So many directions, so at the mercy of others, and my house is so empty and lonely. Everyone seems to have a purpose and plans. I used to have plans. Now, I just don't know. I just don't know where I fit in, if I fit in with anyone, or any place. Nothing feels right, and I don't know how to make it right. I miss talking to my love, figuring things out. No one wants to hear my struggles. There is really no one who cares. Everyone has their life, and I just don't any more. I find moments here and there. Moments that shine, but the polish seems to wear off quickly. Will time fix that? I don't know. It all feels rather empty and pointless today and hard. Just so hard.

It is hard; grief is hard work. And it is that work, not time, that will help soften our grief. Seeing that there are these little moments that shine lets you know that you are doing grief work. Good for you. But it's hard work. Remember to give yourself permission to rest, to give yourself space from the hardness of grief. Be kind to yourself today. You are worth it.

I'm doing better, I really am. I can go through a whole day and get things done and not think too much and go to sleep and normally sleep. And I'm feeling like I'll be OK. And then, I'm doing some work on the computer, and as I'm checking a few things, I don't know what I push, but an email from my spouse, my deceased spouse, is staring at me. Just staring at me as I turn to cold stone. I am frozen. I can't see anything except the name, his kisses to me, his concern and love, sweet words, and I remember. I remember. I remember my love's kisses, the touch, the fragrance, the smile. And it all comes rushing over me that my sweetheart is gone. And all my work, all my days that were going OK just disappear. Gone. And I am sobbing again, the words blurring on the screen. I blindly push keys, bang on the keys, wanting to read more, to touch my love again, feel the warmth, be close, tears are blurring my vision and catching in my throat, and inadvertently I hit a button, a key, and it's gone. My love is gone. Again. He's gone again. Again, and again and again and again. And there is no end. I slam the computer shut. Shit. Anger isn't a strong enough word for how I feel. I am betrayed. A trick played on me. There on the screen, gone from the screen, from my life, from our life. I hate him. I hate him.

I HATE HIM!!!!

Yes, in this moment, you hate everything about this, and yes, even your love. One moment feeling the tenderness of your love, remembering those precious touches, kisses, smiles...and the next, deep, deep anger/rage. You were left. Your thoughts don't care about the truth, that he "died"; you have been thrown into chaos, and there is nothing that will make sense of this — oh, the frustration. Oh, the anger. Oh, the rage.

Yes, right now, I feel nothing but rage, RAGE!!

It's so hard.

Orange Moment

I am having a very difficult time these days. I really didn't know I had this many tears inside me, they seem endless. And people comment that I look so good and am doing so well. They just have no idea what is going on inside me, and that doesn't help. I am working and doing things as suggested by books and by people, but the sadness is crippling me. I just can't get away from myself and this emptiness. I seem drawn to the edge of the hole so often. I am also confused when I speak with people, since everyone has a different view of those who have died, and I refuse to accept that he is gone. He might not speak in ways I was used to, but I do believe he speaks in other ways. I do feel him around, especially in quiet moments. This helps but does not seem to reduce my sadness. I need to find some way to connect the dots here, because I feel like the rug has been pulled out from under me. I question everything and feel like I have lost the point of things. I've lost myself too.

Indeed, you truly have had the rug pulled out from under you. Everything as you knew it, even your sense of yourself, has been shaken and changed and in a sense been tossed into the air. What feels solid now? You know how to work, smile, drive, walk...robotically. And to others, that may look like you are doing "so well." But you know it's not really you. Your whole being is longing to find places that feel familiar and firm.

How precious that you can feel your loved one speak to you and feel his presence. Yes, it helps, but it won't take away your deep sadness right now. Sit with those quiet moments; they will begin to expand and become some of the solid ground your heart needs. Yes, you are a bit lost in this strange world of grief, and that's OK.

I am. That is exactly how I feel......lost.

The house is just soooo big. There are so many rooms. So much lawn to cut. A vegetable garden to keep up. Weeding of flowerbeds. And I'm so isolated out here. And yet he's here. I don't want to move, but I don't feel I have a choice, not really. Not sure I can keep it up myself. Not sure I can pay the bills on one salary. But he's here. This was our place together. I don't want to move. I feel like I'm being pressured by others to make this decision now. And I guess I will have to soon. I'm told if I wait too long, the market won't be in my favour. That was always something he would have looked after. I organized and took care of the money, but he was good at contracts and things like that. We made a good team. And I can't keep two vehicles, but I don't want to let his go. Just seeing it sitting in the driveway gives me comfort. I don't know what to do or how to do it or when to do it or who I ask for help. I don't know what to do. Oh, God, I wish he was here and none of this happened. That maybe I'll still wake up from this awful, awful nightmare.

It is a hard time to make such big decisions. Grief can make just about anything feel overwhelming. At the same time, like you said, there is a reality that is making decisions like this unavoidable and necessary. And by making the decision to move, you know you are making a decision to feel more grief — the grief of leaving the place where you were together. Grief upon grief.

Remember to be kind and patient with yourself. It will be important for you to make a plan that is manageable. Break the tasks down into smaller pieces and prioritize them. It seems that you are finding that he is with you, no matter where you are. I suspect you will find that to be true, no matter where you live. In the meantime, this is a double grief moment, and that's hard.

Creating a plan will help you.

Blank Page Suggestion:
What does your plan look like? Try to get it started.

79

I have decided to stop asking questions that no one can answer. It's making me sick. Literally sick. And even If I get an answer, it won't help. It won't bring him back. At this point…isolation equals isolation. Somehow, I must come to terms with this awful life now. How do I protect myself? If I have to be here, I don't want to be sick and weak and tired every single day.

What do I do?

This work of grief is exhausting. It has assaulted your body as much as your heart and mind. Your body is working so hard to just keep going and at the same time support you as you grieve. Right now, you may need to reduce what's on your plate — let your body take long rests. Eat the things that help bring back some strength. Take long quiet walks. Breathe. Touch base with your doctor, find supplements…you know what to do to help your body heal as you come to understand this different life you have entered into.

I can watch TV now. Well, sometimes. I can sit and concentrate for longer periods of time and actually process **what is happening** *Well, sometimes. Someone suggested watching a popular series that was light and fun, and so I did. I sat down with a cup of tea and found the show on Netflix. And I was very positive and hoped to be taken away for a short time. I can drift into sadness so quickly. The show began, and I liked the characters, was concentrating on the storyline, and then this handsome man came into the scene and was the love interest of the heroine. It was charming, and I was doing all right, until she said his name. It was the same as my love. Who was dead. And I froze. The tea came right back up, and I was spitting it out, choking as I fought to get up and get to the bathroom, where I stood leaning on the sink, tears crashing into the porcelain, white knuckles on the edge of the sink, breath coming in short, quick bursts. I was scared. Images of my deceased husband couldn't enter my mind fast enough; they were smashing into each other. I thought I was going to pass out. I just stood there. Trying to breathe. Knowing it would be some time now before I felt safe enough to turn on the TV again. Hating everything.*

It is so hard when you had hoped to have a moment of relief from your grief and then, without warning, it's broken and your grief feelings and memories flood over you. And once again, you are reminded of how fragile and delicate you are right now. Your whole being is hyper-aware of anything that reminds you of your love; each one of your senses is so keen right now that his name, a song, a book, a movie, a path, the smell of coffee, and a million other things can be a trigger. In time, you will find it won't happen so often. Your world was full of him; your world is still full of him.

Yes, it is.

I walk my dog along the same path that I walked with my husband, a narrow path in the bush behind our house. The dog would merrily skip along, running back and forth to explore and then come back for kisses. My sweetheart would look straight ahead with that cheeky little smile on his face and extend his hand to me. I would slide my hand into his, and he would stop, pull me close, kiss me quickly and then walk on...like a dance step. He was playful like that. He made me laugh and feel young and playful and happy. No wonder the dog bounced around like he did; walking with my husband made me want to bounce around too. As I walk that path now, even the dog has ceased to bounce. The playfulness has slipped out of our lives, like his hand slipping out of mine. But there are moments when I walk quietly that all of a sudden, I have this urge to reach out my hand, like he is beside me, presenting me with his hand to hold. And so, I reach out my hand in the space between and grasp his formless hand and smile. There's no dance step, no quick kiss, not the playful grin. But he's there, he's walking with me. I feel a sense of calm come over me. And I know I am not alone. Oh my god, I miss him so very, very much. Every second is an effort, an eternity. I just try to do my best until I can really be with him again in the same form. I want him back. I WANT HIM BACK.

He gave you so much to miss. I can picture you two walking together with the dog bouncing around you. How brave of you to walk that path again. It's hard, and, at the same time it's a place of connecting with this memory, with him.

I can understand how much you want him back.

Thank you.

I feel tired of the world. Tired of crying silent tears that are recognized by no one. Silent tears that fall out of my eyes and make lines down my face as they drop to the floor, one tear at a time. They move no one. Others are impervious to my pain. They only want to see their own chaos, no room for another's. Even if recognizing another's grief may shift our own, give a different perspective. But that would mean stepping outside of themselves. Terror. The unknown. And so, my silent tears slip down my face, and I feel broken. My calm patience, my desire to disengage, my ability to stay in my own space and contain my pain is broken. I am affected by another. Loud voices, cruel voices and tone, they are like small bullets rapidly being shot in my direction until finally a piece of the wall starts to crumble, and then I am done. I am back in grief. It has wrapped its filthy, selfish arms around me again. And I hate it.

Remember when you heard a time would come when your grief would be contained? You would be protected behind a wall of your own construction.

But then a piece of that wall gets broken down, and it shocks you, disappoints you. Oh, how you hate it. Because you are back there. Back there in the feelings. And those precious, salty, lonely, dripping tears...the voice of your loss, have all returned. AGGHHH.

You had found a way to be relieved of grief. That wall gave you relief. The wall is part of your grief journey. It's helping you take a break from the intensity, the insanity. It's OK. Yes. Grief has wrapped its arms around you again. It has let the world in, the world that is not sensitive to the fragile, little you. Oh, how you hate it all over again.

But how is it part of the journey? This awful painful journey that I never asked for. And what about these people that don't want to hear, too afraid of what grief is. What about the bullets they shoot at me with their insensitive voices and words? What about that?

You are discovering that there are some people who will not be "safe" for you as you grieve and some who just are not safe, period. It's all right to pull back from them — to use your grief-wall to protect your grieving heart. You will also discover that there are others who are "safe," people who will be with you in ways that help. And if you feel there are no safe people right now, if it's only this book you are holding in your hands right now, that's OK too. This book helps you and keeps you safe.

Right now, your wall is needed.

Fine, I'll be careful and rebuild my wall. It's safer in there.

"It's the most wonderful time of the year"... it's everywhere right now. Jingles on commercials, people on movies, sitcoms, talk shows, radio programs, posters, songs in banks...you just can't escape the most wonderful time of the year. It used to be marvellous, true. But now, I really just want to hide until January fourth. The lights and decorations, food and parties are just all too much. Doesn't anyone realize how painful this can all be for many, many people? My husband used to hang the wreath, and so every wreath I see brings tears to my eyes. There was always so much laughter with everything he did. I never remember him being impatient at all. He'd get out the ladder, and I'd hand him the tools, usually the wrong ones, and the wreath. Then we'd do the lights. It all still stings, pulls on my heart like a violin that can play music again, but the strings are too taut, ready to snap, and the sound isn't quite right. That's me, not quite right. My being is filled with numb reminders. My husband used to say to the kids, "Twenty sleeps to Santa," and that was the countdown. Now, it feels like twenty sleeps until the acute pain of daily brightness and constant reminders that he is gone will be over. Until next year. My being has learned to house pain in all forms. Holidays are clearly the worst. And now, "the most wonderful time of the year" will be stuck in my head all day. My husband — he was wonderful, he is wonderful, he always will be wonderful. I love you, my husband. That is wonderful. But this is not wonderful. Not at all. I hate that song.

Yes, he was, he is wonderful and made that song wonderful. But the song hasn't changed. Holidays and anniversaries, the days on the calendar that once held joy now bring dread. It's like the calendar has become an enemy. Thinking of ways to reduce the dread, reduce the intensity, will be important. Can you think of things that will help you through this not-wonderful time of the year?

Not going anywhere, for one. Not watching the movies or hearing the music. Maybe I'll just watch an action movie over and over again so there are no surprises, and nothing with a holiday theme. What do you think?

Having no surprises is a good idea. And if you get bored of that movie, watch another action movie, whatever works. You have learned that this year you don't want surprises, so that's the way to approach any plan that may come your way. And this is OK. Good for you.

Thanks.

Yellow
Moments

Yellow Moment

One year ago today he died.
It's like a black mark on the calendar.
I can't even get out of bed.
I'm not going to.
I'm pulling the covers over my head and staying here. Maybe forever.

Indeed, it is a black mark on the calendar.
It's a hard day — the day that made the black mark on the calendar.
Let the covers shelter you and hold you.
Let it be the day that you stop; let it be what you need it to be.
Today.

I ventured out to find a birthday card for my friend. As I stood at the rack of cards, all I could see were cards for spouses, partners. Suddenly, I couldn't see cards for anyone else. "I love you," Thank you for..." "You make my life..." "What makes a rose and a..." "For the only love..."

I ran from the store in sobs.

That's so hard.

You have become more comfortable with venturing out. Remember when it was next to impossible to leave your house? And sometimes it's little things like the writing on a card, or a song, or a colour, or a smell...and that's all it takes. The little things that we never think about until it happens. And it will happen. You are never far from your love; you are never far from your loss; you are never far from little things.

The next time you venture into the card section, you will know what to do!

What is that?

Think about it for a minute.

OK, well, if I was in a store and that feeling came over me, I would walk out. What do you think?

Perfect!

94

It seems to me that after the moment of waking up from the long grief sleep, as if from a fairy-tale kind of sleep, I am plunged into the next world of grief. The grief of the new reality. I am caught. Suddenly things are sharp and keen, and yet I am keenly aware of the fact that my life is gone. Simply, it just isn't there any more. The castle is empty. Really empty. The life that I had in that castle is gone, the people are gone, the garden has grown wild and thick, and in many ways, I don't want any of it. Problem is, I can't just run away; someone has to look after the castle, and I don't really know where I would go anyway...or what I want to do. And a huge depression falls upon me as the new grief mingles with the old. The loss is even more punctuated than before. And now that I have reached out to others, let some into my space, kissed a prince, everything feels split open, raw, unknown. It becomes brutally clear that everyone has carved their space, and moats around castles are not easily navigated.

Tears find their way into my eyes again, and I curl into a ball...knowing that sleep won't help, knowing there is really no one there for me, no one to help with these monumental decisions. With this new grief. I have to make some really, really hard choices. But how? How? And where do I possibly begin!

Remember when it felt like there was a veil or blanket of grief over everything? You felt like you could hardly breathe under that blanket. But that blanket was protecting you from seeing and feeling and knowing everything about your loss all at once — a blanket that you needed. And now the blanket is slowly lifting, you are beginning to see more and see your loss in a way that you weren't ready to see it before. You have learned ways to help yourself and care for yourself and have gained some energy back, so the blanket isn't needed quite so much. You are right; it's an awakening into the reality of your loss. It's a different kind of sadness. A new kind of grief.

Depression makes it hard to make very hard choices and big decisions. Again, remember to be kind to yourself. Try to reduce what needs to be dealt with to the minimum. Remember too that this will not be the best time to make monumental, life-changing decisions. Talking decisions through with a friend or health-care provider will be important when decisions need to be made. Don't do this yourself. Not now. And, you know, it's OK to make a few mistakes along the way. Be kind to yourself in this new reality of your loss.

It doesn't feel OK, but I see your point. Yes. I won't make any big decisions right now. Things are too fuzzy. Unclear. And I will consult a few people before making any big choices. Good advice...again!

What is the flip side of grief? Grief shrouds me in a dark and heavy cloak. It makes it impossible to breath or eat or feel. I am a prisoner inside a dimly lit room. And then I find a way to pull back the cloak just a little bit, and a ray of light splinters inside. I think grief fights to keep me inside. There is great power in darkness, and it takes time to remember there is more than this dark place. Keeping me there gives grief power over me, and it is a formidable foe. The world is full of darkness and pain; it is easy to sink into that, curl into a ball, and keep the covers over my head. But once that splinter of light pierced into the cloaked spaces, I began to question, and I began to want more. More of that light, more of myself, more breath, more energy, more love, more, more, more. And grief can't give me that. What is the flip side of grief? I'm not completely sure what to call it, so that is what I will explore now. Because I have been touched by that splinter of light and am now curious where it will lead. I want more than the smothering staleness of grief. The flip side. I wonder.

That's an interesting question. Words that might describe the opposite of the symptoms of grief come to mind: hopeless — hope; sorrow — joy; fear — peace... But do they really describe what it means not to be in grief? Perhaps it depends on the words we use to describe our own personal grief: you have used the word dark. Perhaps the opposite for you is light.

Light. Yes. I like that. Things getting lighter, brighter.

Grief can hold us tightly in its clutches, isolating us from self and others. But there are moments in between. I was invited to join a large group of people, all having lost someone close to them, for a special holiday gathering to honour and remember those who had died. At a time when joy should abound, it is in thin order for many. I am not a joiner, never have been. My husband and my boys, and then just my husband was more than enough for me. But with his death, I am forced to walk through different doors, doors I would never have even considered standing in front of before. And so I said I would attend.

As I sat by myself in the room, in a chair at the very, very back, the room slowly filled. There were five white Christmas trees twinkling with white lights around the room. There was a stage with microphones and a screen at the back with snowflakes projected upon it and words reminding everyone that entered that each person's grief is unique. People of all ages found their seats. The word "HOPE" was on the walls around us. Not joy. Hope. And then the ceremony began. I was worried how I would respond to being part of this much grief and sadness; mine alone was hard enough. A Christmas carol was sung to warm the room, but I continued to sit, finding it too hard to sing, and pencilled small drawings in my sketchbook.

A young woman sang a heartbreaking song about Christmas not being the same without her loved one, and my grief welled up. I drew a more detailed sketch in my little book, struggling to keep myself together. The pain was hard. And then I opted to put the sketchbook away and sit in my sadness. Suddenly I could feel my husband standing beside me, there was that familiar tingle on my skin, and soon the room was not only filled with the people in chairs, but all their lost loved ones...children, husbands, wives, mothers, fathers, sisters, brothers, aunts, uncles, friends...their spirits were very present. The energy in the room was electric, like these spirits were all pained by the grief in their loved ones, watching through a one-way glass window where they could see us but we couldn't see them. We could only feel them. The room was bursting with sadness, but also with love that defied physical boundaries. Hope.

And then the names of those in attendance were read to honour them, and their loved one who had died... "We are here with Mary as she remembers her partner Robin and the names and relationships constantly changed. I was terrified when it was my turn to speak, but I did it and it brought a peace to my heart as I spoke the words out loud. As names were read, it was as if lights were turned on all over the room. Small ornaments that had been made in advance with the loved one's name upon it were brought to each survivor. I held mine in my hand, and it was like I was holding him. It was a bit surreal. "We read out the names of those who used to sit beside you, so they will be remembered," and now I was crying. The chair beside me was painfully empty. Images of my husband danced in my mind, his wonderful face, his wonderful eyes, how he would squeeze my hand no matter where we were... My face was wet with tears. We were given small candles that were lit as the overhead lights went off. The thread on my grief sweater was being pulled. I was being unravelled. "Silent Night" was being sung. Seen and unseen worlds collided. Magic. I didn't want to blow out my candle; it was like extinguishing him all over again. I felt a moment of panic.

Then the electricity in the room spoke to me, and I realized there would be nothing I could ever, ever do to extinguish his light. Never. His light will shine forever, and I just have to stand in the right place to be in its glow, like seeing the sun playing behind the trees in a forest and finding that one spot where the sun bathes you in its brilliance...it's finding that spot.

There was a power in coming together with a group of people who really got it, who understood all this grief, and who were brave enough to share together. It's not easy to find true community in grief, but it was here this evening. Another door has been opened.

Oh, my. The courage you had to walk into that room. That was huge for you! You found a way — sitting at the back, having your sketch pad, being still and quiet — a way that helped you be able to be in the room. I am overwhelmed by the beauty that you were able to see in a time that could have been so heavy and dark. You saw hope and light. Everyone in that room felt weak in their grief, and yet in the coming together, there was a power and strength and real hope and the realization that relationships can never be extinguished. No, it's not easy to find a community in grief. Remember we have talked about safe places, safe people. You were open to see if this would be safe for you. You came prepared to leave if you needed to, but open at the same time. You decided, as the evening unfolded, that it was not only a safe place but also a place that could allow your grief to unravel, that there are safe people and safe places. You found that the light of your love is now a part of you forever, never to be extinguished. Yes, another door has been opened.

Thank you.

I don't know what to do with his clothes. I can't keep all his clothes and coats and shoes and boots and hats. He loved his hats. He had summer fedoras, winter ones with feathers running back from the brim, caps for summer made of straw, sexy hats, funny hats for gardening. Great hats. They are sitting on the shelf, waiting for him still. I let my sons wear a few, but some are too sacred to me, and when I hold them close, I can still smell him. I couldn't give away all his clothes either. The t-shirts he loved, the shirt he wore when we got married, the jeans with the rip on the knee. Wow, he had such a great ass in a pair of Levi jeans. Can't throw those out. He had one wool sweater that he really loved, wore it every day, and if I wrap it around me and close my eyes, it holds his scent so sweetly, I can almost pretend he's holding me. I won't put it on, I don't want it to take on my fragrance. I know his scent will fade with time, but the fibres are holding him fast, and I keep it in a place in my closet. I don't want to let it go. I never want to let it go. His dark blue terrycloth robe hangs there, limp without his burly form inside. I will put that on and wrap it around me. I miss him. I want him back. And those leather sandals. Just can't part with them. They will stay in the closet too. Along with his runners, his winter boots, his work boots. As I go through the closets, I realize I don't want to throw any of it out. But I know I can't keep it. It's agony to open any closet. He's there but not there. I don't know what to do with his clothes. Help me.

The closet, the clothes are agony. They seem to call for a decision. To keep or not to keep! Making it a more gentle decision may help. You certainly don't need to get rid of everything that holds connection and meaning for you. There may be another closet in your house that can hold his things for now, so they aren't in your face every time you reach for a piece of your own clothing. Or sorting through things if you're ready; not to purge, just to reduce. It's about finding what will work for you and what will be kind to you. A balance.

And for now, the closet may remain just the way it is — and that is OK.

Let me think about it. Thanks for helping me find my way and giving such great options.

I'm glad that helped. You are learning what works for you. I'm so glad.

Seems like once you are a widow, others feel you are hot to trot and very available. I am hardly available in any way at all.

It has pained me that men have approached me and asked me to dinner. They were polite and jovial when my husband was alive but never indicated any desire for something more. Now I appear to be fair game. Have they no idea what's happening? Do they not know I still love him and feel devoted to him?

I didn't realize I had built-in protection with my husband beside me. And when they ask and I reply, in quiet disbelief, and tell them that I could never go out, my husband was the only man for me — they laugh. They laugh right in my face. I find this not just insulting, but embarrassing. It is another reason to stay hidden away. It makes me miss my husband even more.

I am a very affectionate, physical person. I hug people in the European way. That seemed to be OK when my husband was alive, but now it says that I am forward and asking for something. I don't get it. Even a colleague who came to visit. I thought he would arrive with his daughter and dog. But he came alone and bearing flowers. I felt uncomfortable but just filed it away as we women are good at doing. Little pats on my arm and my hand made me bristle through the afternoon. And then when he left, a hug that pressed my breasts against him and a kiss just below my ear was not European style. I stepped back, and my dog rushed over to save the day. I smiled robotically and waved goodbye. I was rattled. I don't know how to be in the world any more. I miss my husband. I feel very exposed. I want my husband back. I'm a bit scared.

I'm so sorry you are having these experiences. Sadly, this is the reality for many when someone they've loved dies. You may even find someone saying to you, "Just find someone else and that will make you feel better." They don't have any idea. It's a time when you are vulnerable and lonely. And once again, you have to put up that little wall to create safe space to continue your healing journey. Your innocence is gone. You are seeing that you have to become your own protector. And your grief antennae are now tuned into this new development. This experience taught you. Now you are aware.

You're right. People have said that to me, "It's OK, you'll find someone new." I feel like punching them. How can they say that? It's like saying that person is as easy to replace as a car. It's so cruel. Heartless. I don't know how people can hook up so quickly with someone new. Makes my stomach turn a little bit.

It is interesting to see how different people navigate their loss journey. Remember how unique your relationship and your loss is — it's totally personal. Someone else's may be different to the point where they are ready to be in relationship. Or it may be a way to fill a void or feel less scared. Remember that we can't compare our journey with someone else's. You can only listen to yourself. You are making wise choices for YOU.

Right. Stay focused on myself. And protect myself, if that's what I need. I feel it's what I need.

Small children drag their dolls or teddy bears behind them, holding on to one arm that slowly pulls the stitching out. The doll's head drags on the floor or bounces on the edge of staircase steps going up and down. The doll is squashed into a corner on the couch, often sat on or pushed under a pillow. It is forced to listen to stories it dislikes, music it hates, movies that are offensive, and taken places it doesn't want to go. At bedtime it is dragged under the covers and inevitably, during the night, it falls out of the bed, onto the floor, slides under the bed, and is forgotten for a number of days. It lies there collecting dust. When it is eventually found and dusted off, it will be dragged around by the arm again or put on a shelf because while it was lost, another doll replaced it. Grief is the child. I am the raggedy doll.

Grief does seem to drag us around, doesn't it? Drag us unwillingly into places and experiences that we would rather avoid. Yes, grief does that.

As we begin to grow with grief, as it becomes more known, the raggedy doll becomes what it has always been...something you can hold on to for comfort and warmth. Just beautiful!! That's you. Beautiful. You know that, right?

Yes, young grief drags us around, for a while.

So how do I maintain myself when I feel like I am outside my body and want to be with someone...I want to touch someone, talk, laugh. I am human, I need interaction. But it means walking through that door. Instead, I find myself waiting. Watching. If I just stand in the door frame, I can turn around and go back. I haven't committed, haven't walked through. How do I keep myself intact standing betwixt and between? I feel my love guiding me through these very sharky, unfamiliar waters. But I am still alone. I guess I could stand in the doorway, just stand there and watch. But I can't feel anything in the doorway. I am just part of the door. And I could go back, but to what...my chair? It's funny how death follows, nips at my heels, pulls me back. But grief is a shapeshifter. And I am shifting. I feel different in my skin. Will I get hurt again if I walk through certain doors? Will things be taken away again? Will I fall into the abyss? I don't know. But I can't stand in the doorway forever. There is nothing in the doorway...no forward, no back. Every doorway is unknown now. Scary.

It is a scary place — that place in between the immediacy of your loss and when you begin to move. Pause here. Look how far you have come from your chair. Think about the ways you helped yourself and listened to your own pace and heart. These same ways of finding your way will be the ones that you will use as you move through this doorway. And the next. And the next. The reminders of unbelievable loss keep you on guard and wary, and yet you can feel the pull and are becoming ready for little risks of connection. Yes, indeed, it is a scary place. It is also the place of wonder and shapeshifting. When you are ready, little baby steps close to the door.

Ok I want to step through this doorway, I really do. But am I ready?

Yes, you are ready.

Blank Page Suggestion:
Tell me some things you would like to find on the other side of the door.

109

I'm sad today. My house feels infinitely empty. Sometimes it feels like the hole that was left by my love is so huge, I will never find a way to fill it. There are many, many days when the sun shines and I feel him close to me, but I have to work at that, and things all need to be in a good place. Many things have been out of place in the last few days, and it weighs upon me more heavily with him gone. Some days, like today, I find it difficult to get out of bed, and I wonder if we all just live to die. And maybe we do, really, but it's what we do in between the birthing and the dying. Today, it's hard to know what to do with the in-between. It feels like just filling space and time for no apparent purpose. There was purpose with my sweetheart here. In an odd way, I'm not really sure why it felt so different then. It is hard to find words for so much of this, a time when language is faulty and scarce. Incomplete. Thin. And big questions arise — what are we doing here, what is the point of anything. I guess when my love was here, we meant so much to each other that it was the sharing of experience, really. Someone special to brainstorm ideas with, someone to be upset with, laugh with, love with, share dinners and music with, sunsets, successes, failures, next steps. Someone to notice me, mark me. Now I come home to an empty house and there is no one here to share with. Empty. A tree hit by lightning now stands hollow with woodpecker holes and broken branches. What can possibly be next for that tree? Is there a next? I am sad and disheartened today.

The picture of the tree being hit by lightning — what a powerful image of what you have been going through. You are left with gaps and questions and emptiness. And "empty" is a hard place to find answers or energy or direction or purpose. Empty is just empty. This is where you are today: sad and disheartened. And that is OK. In this tender time, it is the little things of looking after yourself that will help. Sitting in your favourite chair, staring out the window, a hot drink, a blanket around your shoulders, comfy clothes, keeping warm, tucked into bed. Empty invites us to stop.

All right. I'll stop, try to find the good in empty. I hear what you are saying. Sometimes that's all I can do. Readjusting my concept of empty. I'll work on it. Thanks for getting it.

I do.

I wish I could take back every single unkind word I ever spoke to him. Every silly fight we had. I wish I could go back and fix those moments, know that I never made him sad or feel bad. It kills me that I ever hurt him. I so wish none of those moments had happened. That I hadn't been in a bad mood. That I hadn't lashed out at him because I didn't like something else. We did have so many beautiful moments, but now I can only think of how many were wasted, ruined. I would give anything to have those back and do it again. Let him know how much I loved and valued him.

I should never have spoken an unkind word to him. These thoughts are tormenting me. I can't escape them. I am riddled with guilt.

It can be hard to recall hard words and fights. Healthy relationships need space for these times so that you can grow as individuals and in your love. That's what love looks like. Those fights and hard words you wish you could take back now were part of the true fabric of your relationship. You wouldn't want to go back and change any of it. Regret doesn't really help, does it?

After a fight or hard words, you would have had a conversation together. Would you like to tell me or even write out what it is you would like to say to him about the ones you are remembering and didn't have a chance to talk about? Think about how he would reply. Maybe that can clear things for you.

Yes, I like that idea. It's a good one. There are a few I can remember where we didn't really get a chance to talk after. I'll write down what I wanted to say, and I'll write his response as well. Yes, it helps to even think about it. Thanks. I want to do that now. You're right, regret brings me nothing but a stomach-ache.

Regret can do that — bring stomach-aches. As you write, as you talk with him, your stomach will begin to settle. You have a lot of courage to be still and remember. Good for you. That's a big step.

Today I saw how grief haunts me, follows me, stalks me, really. But I also discovered there is no one to call, no 911 number to save the day, rescue me, help me. No one but me. And me is a little tired. Tired of feeling alone, inadequate, unsure, scared. Tired of my brain producing difficult thoughts that hurt my stomach and send my heart racing. Today I learned that two parts of my brain don't really communicate, they cause trouble for me, and are not easily swayed or shifted. Today I learned that my panic needs to be soothed by me, and I don't really know how to do that. Today I learned that I am very, very young. Today I learned I am mother, sister, friend, aunt, and maybe even grandmother to myself. But today I also learned that I wish it all wasn't true. That joy was easier to hold. Easier to find. Easier to keep. Today I learned that grief is a true enemy. Although I feel I have fought to stand up and walk and change and feel and taste, I also feel that I sit in exactly the same spot as when he died, and I wish it wasn't true.

Even when you have some supportive people around you the reality is you can feel alone in your grief. No one can actually be in that place with you. It does feel like a fight: a fight to stand, or walk, or do most of the things that took no effort before he died. It's a hard reality.

Is that what you mean by "grief is a true enemy"? That it feels like it is a constant fight?

No, that I am on constant watch, being stalked, on guard, hunted, in danger.

Hypervigilant, because it came at you out of the blue, no warning. Your world feels like a place full of danger. Death reminds you that you don't have control.

Am I all alone then?

Yes and no. You will have moments when the voice of your loved one is with you. And you will have moments when you feel understood by someone that has experienced loss and feel that connection. And then there will be moments where there is no other voice but your own. You will learn how to trust yourself, be your own comfort, and find that soothing moment we have spoken about. You can do it.

When I went to get the mail the other day, there was an envelope addressed to my husband. My hand shook a bit as I took it out of the mailbox. Odd feeling. It was like he would just be in the house and I'd hand it over. I felt caught between two worlds again. My eyes filled with tears as I began to open the envelope. I wiped the tears away with my sleeve so I could see what was inside. Driver's license renewal. I laughed out loud in a manic sort of way, incredulous about the heartlessness of government. They hounded and hounded me when he died for documents and money, and yet they couldn't update the system so these notices would stop. Grief is selective. Not everyone is aware. Most don't even care. I realized then how many notices I was going to receive over the course of the year. I thought I'd be ready. But then the hydro bill came with both our names on it. I broke down again. It was like each time a piece of mail came with both names on the front, or just his, it was like a notice saying I had dreamt it all. And there was always this surreal moment where I thought it might be true. Grief makes no sense. It seems to span time and space and consciousness. Nothing makes sense! What have we been taught and conditioned to believe. I had called the hydro company a few times already, and nothing changed, so I decided I would leave it. I still felt we shared everything together. Just because the physical body was gone didn't mean his presence and energy didn't still circle around me. We created our place together and put our name on things together, so I decided I would see the monthly hydro bill as a reminder that my love was still here and helping me. Not gone. The name in black and white on the envelope window attested to that. And every piece of mail I get with his name on it will be a constant reminder to me that my love is here with me. But what happens when mail for my love doesn't arrive any more? What then?

You found a brilliant way to cope with the reality of mail. At first it knocked you off your feet and challenged your reality. It led you to frustration at the heartlessness of government. And then you were able to turn this into — is this the right word? — a gift of remembering and the constant reminder that your love is with you. Good for you!

And what will happen when the mail doesn't arrive any more? I suspect you will go through a process, just like this one, that will lead you to a new way of coping with that new reality. You are trusting the process; you are trusting yourself!

So, the mousetraps my husband set before he died caught a mouse. OMG. I went to the neighbour, and she said her husband wouldn't be home for a few days. There would be an awful stench by then. Death and grief reeked. So, it was up to me. I silently cursed him for setting those traps as I tried to decide what to do. He was so good at everything. I never realized how much he did. Sometimes he used live traps, sometimes he didn't. Clearly, he hadn't this time. I went and got my husband's very large work gloves; they went up to my elbows. They were leather and cloth so very heavy. You had no sensitivity in your hands, couldn't feel a thing, which was the point. Then I went and got his longest BBQ tongs. I didn't like BBQ'ing much anyway. Next a plastic bag and my sunglasses — I didn't really want to see this thing too easily. So, there I am, gloves and tongs in place as I solemnly walk toward the carcass. I reached around the corner, squinting so I couldn't really make out anything but the trap, dark blue with a red handle that executed the occupant. It was a reusable trap — yah, sure. Like I'm going to take this creature out and reuse the trap.

Even though it was a mouse, I hated being around death. It seemed to have permeated my skin. I reached over with my tongs, but they kept slipping off and dropping the trap. I had to bend down lower and grab the trap right at the bottom in order to get it to the plastic bag. Traps have to be set near the wall and around a large object like a water heater or a fridge, said my husband. "Mice run along the walls," I could hear him saying. "Shut up," I yelled at him, "you've left me with this disaster. You know how I hate this. Shut up. Shut up. You have nothing to say here. You are gone. You left me with a mess."

The trap was really awkward to reach. I grabbed it again and slid it along the floor and into the open. I stopped, panting. I made the mistake of taking my sunglasses off to wipe the sweat off my forehead with the sleeve above my elbow, or maybe it was tears running out the tops of my eyes as I was bent over, hard to know. Either way, the moment I took off the sunglasses, there was the dead mouse staring at me with his tiny little black eyes fixed right onto my face. He was dead, true, but his eyes were larger than life and piercing. I forced myself not to cry, because then I knew the job would not get finished. I put my sunglasses back on, holding my breath now, wet spots on the lenses making it even harder to see, and picked up the tongs, squinted, and grabbed the trap, flipping it into the plastic bag.

I put down the tongs and stepped well back from the bag so it was just within reach of my fingers in the large gloves. I gingerly picked up the bag between two fingers and held it at arm's length while I walked to the door, opened it, and tossed the bag out onto the lawn. I leaned against the closed *door, breathing heavily. A tiny little voice in my head said I would now have to buy new traps and set them, because when I tried a live trap and opened it, the door got stuck, I had to hold it so close to my face and then it sprang open and the mouse leapt out. I almost had a heart attack. I hated killing them, but they weren't listening to me pleading for them to stay outside. My back slid down the door, and I landed with a thud on the floor. I sat there for a very, very long time.*

Oh, you were so brave.

So brave. You talked yourself through an extremely difficult situation, one that you never would have had to face if he was still there. You found a way to face this death. I suspect someday you will chuckle at the picture in your mind of you with the sunglasses, huge gloves, BBQ tongs, doing the impossible. You did it.

You must have been exhausted afterward.

I couldn't believe how exhausted. I guess I'll have to learn to set the traps too. Or finally handle the live traps. Agghhh.

I'm sure YouTube has a good video on that...

That makes me laugh.

Grief loves lyrics in songs because it keeps us in grief. When he died, I didn't want any music, he took all the music in me when he died. And we had different music playing all the time in our home. Now, I just wanted silence. Safe silence. But my son said it was the wrong kind of silence. He suggested classical music. It had moments of too much power, which my son quickly adjusted to a more peaceful movement, but it allowed for a soothing of my soul. It created a space where I could rest, in between the screaming pain in my heart and the agony of silence without my love.

I couldn't listen to anything on the radio, especially when driving. News reports were raw like me, and it was a tree crashing into another falling tree. It plunged me into despair, which was very easy. Every song on the radio or on my iPod either had a memory attached or had a phrase that took me back to my love or made me want him back. Love songs killed me, just killed me. I couldn't breathe, couldn't see, and certainly couldn't safely operate a vehicle. It was like the torture of water-boarding... I couldn't get my breath, there were so many tears it was like drowning, I couldn't get away, and really, I just wanted it all to end. This grief was like being put into a straitjacket. How would I ever be able to reorganize my life? How could I ever fit comfortably into my body again? Classical music, especially the cello and the harp, at least allowed the torture to stop for the duration of the song. My son sweetly searched for just the right recordings and brought them home for me. So I decided to have it playing all the time in my house, and it helped. It helped me sit in my body, not comfortably, but at least be in it. It helped me to move around. Do things. It helped to reconnect me, slowly, with the world around me and guided me toward each next step, gently, with no words to distract me or push me off the bus or under it. Thank you, Bach, and Mozart, and Haydn, and Beethoven for soothing me. And a little Jack Johnson here and there.

Thank you Bach, Mozart, and the rest of you! Now that's a big transition for you. Music is powerful, that's for sure. It has had the power to throw you into a deep grief, and, as you have discovered, it has the power to soothe...when you are ready. And now you are ready. At least today you are. You know what you can and can't handle and when you are ready. Awesome.

Blank Page Suggestion:
Write out the lyrics of a song that has spoken to you.

Yellow Moment

Rain is snow
snow is rain
it hangs heavily
on the evergreens
pulling them down
weeping
weighted
hard to pull up
and together

I am listening. I am listening.

One of the things that is a great agony for me is not having anyone to talk to. Being very private, it was always hard for me. And when I do talk, I am usually interrupted and start closing down and feel invisible. My love was always really aware of that and took time to hear me and made others hear me. It's often hard for others to understand that about me. But in myself, I am rather shy; being a champion of others is easier than of self. He was my champion, and he made such a difference. And although I am working hard to find a different path and way of handling all this, it is tricky. Dark thoughts are powerful. I am redirecting them, but it's still tricky. I guess I'm still not really good at it yet. I want to live in the colours, but darkness overcomes so quickly.

And even though I try to replace thoughts of fear, wow, they creep in. I feel scared of the summer…it was our time to really be together in all the things we loved. I'll hopefully be in a different place by then, where I can cope better, but in the meantime, I'm scared.

He truly was your champion. As you have shared stories of him, I have come to see him through your eyes. Your love for each other and the expressions of that love, through listening, through special times and seasons together, made a difference in both your lives. Anticipating moments that you once shared can be scary. Finding ways to be kind to yourself in those times and seasons that were once special will help them be a little less scary. Try to think of something you could plan for the summer. Something you would like to do with a friend. Begin new adventures knowing he would love to see you doing them.

OK. I think I can do that. But what if I have no one who can go with me? What can I plan then?

Remember when we talked about the plans and dreams that you had made together? Perhaps there is short day trip that you could do, solo, that would bring him honour and bring you a planned outing. It may be as simple as taking an art class, going to the theater, an art gallery, a wine tasting. Doing some of the things you enjoy where you know others will also be on their own. What comes to your mind when you think of these kinds of options?

Well, first I think that not too many people do things on their own. I would really stand out. I would like to do a wine tasting.

A wine tasting — what a great idea!

Who knows, maybe there are more people doing things on their own than you realized — you've lived in a "couple" world so long that you may not have noticed. I'm ready to learn about that from you too!

OK. I'm going to look into it. I'm a bit excited now.

Yellow Moment

Thin. I feel thin. Like I could slip between the cracks and disappear. Thin. Like a slip of paper that can fit underneath a door. Thin.

I can't live the life we had. My son has reminded me of my financial situation. I guess I thought it might blow away or magically transform as I slept one night. No such luck. Another side of grief. I have to sell things we both loved, because I can't afford to keep them on one income. I know I can't keep the house. Sure, there was insurance money, but not a lot. Not enough. And most of it paid for the funeral. And the government. But what about day to day, month to month? It's not the same alone. It's like just as I begin to stand up, I'm slapped down again. And again. And again. How much can I take until I just don't want to get up again? I feel very low today. I don't have the answers.

Thin.

Then today is a day not to have answers.
Today is a day for you to be still.
Today is a day to feel thin...and that's OK.
You will find your way; that can be for tomorrow or the next day.
Today is a day to pause.
Can you make a cup of your favourite hot drink?

Yes.

Perfect.

We never got to do our trip to Europe. We were always involved with kids and work and racing from one thing to the other, and renovating and planning that trip. But we never got to do it. We wanted to take the train through Italy and see the art in Venice and Milan. Eat pasta and olives. Drink wine. Make love in Tuscany in a sweet little villa. We never got to do any of that. We never got to take that ski holiday. We researched and planned it. Talked about the hills we would tackle together and ones we would avoid. How we would sip beverages while naked in hot tubs and watch movies in our hotel room snuggled together. Be first on the hill and last off. Lots of talk. But it never happened. I didn't tell him I loved him enough. I didn't tell him how much I loved the flowers he always gave me. I didn't tell him how it filled me with tingles every time he kissed me when he came in the door. How good he smelled. How caring he was. What a great dad he was. And the day he died, we were busy with cleaning things up in the yard, getting ready for winter, and I never said I loved him once that day. And I never got to say goodbye. Never. Never. How do I live with those kinds of regrets? They eat at my core each and every moment.

Yes, grief does tear at your core.

What beautiful, full, and exciting dreams and plans you were making together...things that the two of you looked forward to. Dreaming together is part of a healthy relationship. It sounds like you had fun together, dreaming. Part of your grief journey will be grieving the loss of those dreams, hopes, plans, wishes...another layer of your loss. In time, you will remember the joy that the planning brought you, and you may even choose to complete one of these dreams in his honour. For now...it causes you pain.

Your conversation with him was never completed; there was so much more to say. That's the way your conversations were. Something you may find helpful would be to keep having those conversations, out loud, on paper...things you would like to say, not only about back then, but now. Tell him how you are doing and what's happening for you. You know how he would reply. You know. Write his reply as well. And you can hold that close. Hold him close.

I love that. I'm going to start writing now.

I'm excited for you.

.

Blank Pages for Your Story

Blank Pages for Your Story

132

Blank Pages for Your Story

Blank Pages for Your Story

Blank Pages for Your Story

Green
Moments

I used to love setting the table for dinner. It was just the two of us, but it was grand. He would bring flowers home because he knew how much I loved them. I would have the table all set. He would put my favourite music on. I like a glass of wine; he preferred ale. I had the appropriate glasses at each place setting. We always made it special. Every night. Sometimes the meal was quick, even takeout when we were both really busy, but that was our time to debrief and come together. We would sit across from each other. We would toast to something, light the candles, and talk. With my love gone, I don't really even want to eat, let alone sit at the table. I had started to eat on my lap in a living room chair, in front of the TV, because it was just too hard eating at the table. Even if someone came, it just wasn't the same. A friend of mine suggested that I set a place across from me anyway. She gave me a gift of two plates and two wine glasses. I thought it was kind of creepy at first. But I thought I would give it a try. I made dinner and set another place for my love. And even though the plate was empty, and no one was there to lift a glass, I toasted anyway. Toasted how well we loved each other. Talked out loud about things that had happened that day. Even asked what my love thought. And it was nice to sit at the table again, to talk with him. I didn't tell people I did this; I figured they would look at me strangely, give that "poor her" look and nod, which I just hate. I still had the TV on in the background; otherwise it was just too quiet. I didn't set another place every night. Sometimes I did, sometimes I didn't. But I did set a place for me every night. I began to make dinner special again, just for me. My love would have liked that.

Yes, he absolutely would.

Interesting how this suggestion from your friend, which at first seemed creepy, was something that filled a gap. Once we have been opened to the journey of grief, we discover things that others may think strange or even crazy. Someone may light a candle and sit with a cup of tea and chat with their loved one; another may talk to their loved one as they drive; another may close their eyes and dance in the kitchen like they used to when together. All these are sweet, connecting moments, reminding you that your loved one is forever anchored in your heart.

Beautiful and tender moments. They are your moments. Love them.

It does get easier. Well, sort of. Days when good things happen, when friends are around, when activities and work happily tumble around each other. Grief seems to settle into the background then, foggy. But then there are those quiet moments. The deeply quiet ones. The ones that sneak up on you, like a thief meticulously working the lock to enter your house. Like you are suddenly caught inside a cotton ball. And it is there in the deep silence that the fog lifts and grief is standing front and center. Or when you are feeling sick, not quite on your game, a little run-down, and difficult thoughts seem to dance in your head more readily. In these moments, you are lost in memories and longing; the tools of grief. And the pain and loss and resonance are intense, as if it happened yesterday. Even though it happened years and years ago, or a month ago, or a few years. It doesn't matter, because time is warped by grief. It feels like grief is never that far away.

So true. Grief has become part of the fabric of your life...a tapestry that has threads of loss woven in and changing the picture of who we are. You are reminding us that we never "get over" or "finish" with grief — yes, it softens, and there are good days. And then there are those moments where it's "as if..." as if the loss were yesterday. And our feelings are strong and deep all over again. They can come when we are still and quiet, or they can come by the trigger of a song, or a place, or a smell, or a sound... They may feel bittersweet as for a moment you are connected again with your loved one; and for a moment you feel the depth of the loss all over again.

Like a balloon blowing up as I feel grief rising inside me, then popping, bursting, and then it's done. No more balloon. And the moment of grief passes. OK. It's like learning to walk all over again.

Indeed. Yes, you are learning how to embrace these moments, these balloons, as part of your personal story. As part of your life. Not to fight them or push them away, but to allow them. You may come to find that these moments of grief bring with them a moment of relief as you remember precious moments with your loved one.

Nice to find good tears for a change. Thank you.

I was in the bank the other day, and I pulled out the wrong bankbook. It was ours, with both our names on it. I had removed them both from online banking. It was just my name now, on most things. But I guess this bankbook had been buried in my bag. I was standing there, the bankbook in my hand, the ink bleeding from my tears. And I felt someone standing beside me. I looked up and knew the face. Not well. But I knew the face from having lived in the community a while. The thing that shocked me was she started to speak. "It's been a while now, dear. It would be best to move on from your grieving." I just stared at her and turned and walked out of the bank. How dare she. HOW DARE SHE. With everyone standing around. Holy shit. Does she know my heart? Does she have one of her own? I wanted to go back and slap her across the face. Instead, I got into my car and wept silently. Because now I feel I really can't show my grief in public. Oh, God.

Oh, dear.

Yes, how dare she! But sadly, this kind of response is more common than not in our grief-avoidant society. When you were telling me the story, and you got to the part where you saw a familiar face, I thought, oh good. Instead, the opposite. And the message that you aren't grieving correctly. I'm so sorry this happened to you.

This was a moment that came out of nowhere, and so all the more vulnerable because you weren't expecting it. Remember that there will always be some who will walk away from your grief, some who will try to be present but are afraid of your grief, and those who will come alongside and support you in grief, and some who think they know everything and shoot their mouths off. This is a sad reality. Does knowing that help you think about showing your grief in public?

Hmmm. No, not really. A comment like that kind of threw me under the bus, and it's so hard for me to recover from that. And I thought I was getting better, doing so much better. I guess I'll have to learn how to put on a plastic face when I go out.

Remember early in your grief, when it was hard to step outside your door, let alone go inside the bank...or the grocery store, or hair salon, or anywhere? The grief work you have done has brought you to the place of being able to go there. Yes, you are doing so much better. No guarantees of how it will go; you learned that one the hard way! But remember, her response isn't a measure of how you are doing. Only you make that decision. Keep moving forward. Keep venturing out. You are doing great!

Green Moment

I was given a reprieve. My life had turned a corner, and grief was pushed to the side of the room. It was a fitting place for the crippling guest who I felt was overstaying their visit. And I didn't want to think or talk about grief when I clearly was not feeling too grief-like. And yet even though grief sat to the side, it sadly did not leave and walk out the door, never to be heard from again. It sometimes feels like I'll never be free and that somehow I need to be set free. I'm not quite sure how. The reprieve is over, brief and over, it seems. I liked the reprieve better. It was lighter. So how do we get grief from the side and out the door, never to be seen or heard from again. How?

What if grief were to become something that you didn't feel you had to "fight"? What if you offered grief a chair, not so much on the side, but just in the room? What if you began to think of grief in a different kind of way? Remember when you talked about how grief has changed you and brought new eyes, new depth, new understanding — things that are good. What if grief could be allowed to become good?

Hmmmm. Interesting. Let me think about that.

It's a messy business, this waking up from grief, from loss. Now things are not done over again, it is something done for the first time. First time can be hard. Hard because in many ways I am simply not prepared for outcomes. It's like being young again and venturing out into the wide world with a lot more knowledge in my backpack. Still, a first is a first. First time I walk in that forest since my husband died, first time I have friends stay over, etc., etc. I'm sure there will be hundreds more. And it is refreshing; it is invigorating to do things I never thought I would do again. But it's such a bizarre dichotomy. I wasn't prepared for the fact that when everyone left, there was this infinite space and silence again. Like a boulder rolling in front of the door. It wasn't what my life was to be...these infinite echoes. It was palpable, I could taste it. I sat down and sobbed. I don't think they were tears of sadness so much as of recognition. A first. A realization. So, I regrouped, moved the boulder from the door, went for a walk, and returned to my new self who deals with things. Tries, anyway. No, the space and the silence are OK; they are mine, and that is simply the way it will be for some time, with a sprinkling of visitors and guests to change the echoes. And I will continue to reclaim and reinvent myself until more of the pieces fall into their places. Yes, it's messy. But so is finger-painting, and I love finger-painting.

Messy is a good word for grief, that's for sure. It's not about neat, linear, clean movements from one "stage" to the next, as many in our society would like to believe. Grief turns the world upside down and isn't neat about it. Yes, firsts can be hard, and seconds can be a different hard, and thirds... Hundreds of firsts. Your realization of all that you have learned from grief allows you to regroup and deal with things when these moments come. You are reclaiming yourself. You are also reclaiming the firsts.

Nice.

Grief provides no manual. There should be a covenant with death that manuals are provided for specific tasks performed by the one taken away. How am I supposed to know how to deal with high-tech stereo equipment now that things are breaking and not working when I never had to before... I remember snippets of things he would do, but that doesn't allow me to fix the problem. I can't just throw everything out because I don't know what to do. There'd be nothing left in my house. He'd be on the floor with all his precious tools (God, I hate tools, HATE them) fixing the dishwasher when it acted up, and Bing! the job was done. It's expensive to keep calling repair people. And then the motion sensor light outside needed to be replaced, but when I bought one there was no plug at the end...oh, I'm supposed to wire it in...really? The list gets longer and longer, it seems. I get tired of calling people to help. At that moment, I walked through the door of anger, forgetting my grief. I AM MAD!. How could he just die and leave me with all this? Was there any justice or fairness in the universe at all? Hot tears sting my eyes as I pound my fists on the wall in desperate rage at this twisted and cruel scenario.

All those "little" things that he did which made life run smoothly. The "little" things that can be forgotten until they pop up and remind you all over again that he is not there. Yes, angry for sure. Angry that he is not there to fix all the broken things, including your heart.

Thanks for understanding.

I do, I really do. It's interesting when these strong emotions come back to us with such intensity. It can be surprising. Was it a surprise to you?

A little bit, yes. I thought I was past that intense anger and rage, past those Red moments. But maybe not. Is this how it will always be?

Remember when we talked about how grief is messy, not linear and orderly? This is part of that when out of nowhere there's an "as if" feeling, as if you are "back there" again. But you aren't; you are remembering, with thought and feeling. Any of the intense emotions you have had could pop up again, but they won't linger and grab on to you like before, and you aren't starting over or "back there"...you are remembering. Over time, these moments will soften and reduce in frequency. In the meantime, remember, it's OK. It's OK to feel them, embrace them, own them, and pound a wall.

Will do! Thanks.

Is it really better to have loved and lost than never to have loved or been loved at all? I'm not sure. People who have not lost their love have no right to say this to me. It is haunting me.

I'm so sorry. No, they have no right. Sadly, they don't know any better. What is haunting you?

I don't know, I'm trying to answer that question.

Perhaps that is part of what the grief journey is about...trying to find answers to questions like this...and unfolding into new insight. It's OK, in fact, it's good not to know the answer right now. Let yourself discover it.

That feels a little scary, but it's all kind of scary. And I'm still here. I'll let it simmer for a bit.

Green Moment

New Year's Eve Day. Used to feel like the world was full of options and a resolution was like a magic spell that would set the course of a new day into a new direction. And I will try to still conjure that feeling and image. But without my love to hug and kiss at midnight, with my muse gone, that is a pretty hard task. Still, new beginnings, and I am still here for some reason, however cruel and demented it may be to ask me to do this all alone. But I must try and find my own path now. So, in honour of my love, whom I never want to hurt or disappoint, I will make a resolution and wait to see magic. My resolution is that I will learn to live alone with some kind of lifted spirit (can't ask for joy just yet) and that I will find the new niche so that I can finally begin again. There has to be a path for me to walk that is not filled with tears and loneliness. This year, I want to find that path, whatever, or wherever it may be. So magic...come forth. Lifted spirit New Year to you all. :)

And may it be so for you too. May your spirit be lifted, May the magic be seen, May your path have moments that continue to honour your love...and yourself.

Lifted spirit New Year to you too. :)

Blank Page Suggestion:
What is your New Year's resolution? Note the date so you can check back.

157

Since I lost my love, I have felt like there are pieces of me all over the floors, all over every floor, and all I do is keep sweeping them up into a pile. And I am nowhere. I feel that each one of those pieces is a separate item of grief, and that if I focus on my grief in pieces, small pieces, it is not as life-threatening as dealing with all the grieving pieces at once. And when I've dealt with that one piece of grief, however big or small, it may be ready to find its place in my new self. Because that is what I'm doing, putting myself back together again. I'm just not sure how it will look when it's done. But it's happening one piece at a time. So I am going to try to deal with grief in a way that allows me to find new directions and ways to think and be. And I'll see how that goes, because, to be sure, the other way makes it hard to get out of bed or off the couch or out the door. And I certainly don't want to stay on the couch forever. Grief pieces. Where to start?

You are remembering to be kind to yourself as you look at the pieces of yourself that have been touched by grief: one piece at a time. You have learned to slow things down so that you can manage and not be overwhelmed, allowing yourself to find new direction and learn about how grief has changed every part of you. Good for you!

Where to start? I think you already have. Look at how you are responding to the part of you that is planning to manage one piece at a time.

Green Moment

Grief knows no borders and no religious affiliation. It is a global citizen. A few rather thoughtless people have said to me, "Oh, you'll get over his death, at least you don't live in Syria or Africa, at least you are not a refugee." Oh My God. Grief is a personal crisis, as real and shocking as being plunged into a pool of ice water with no way out. And no one's grief supersedes the other. Personal grief is measured by the depth of love one holds for the deceased, not region or war or ravages. Whether in the Middle East or Africa or North America, grief is a deep, deep hole we face. In many ways, North America offers the least support for one who is grieving. People seem terrified by the pain grief can cause, and so they shy away from those who grieve, isolate them so the affliction won't be passed on. There is no time for grief. A few minutes offered on the phone, a few visits here and there, all offered in between work and shopping and planning for the next event. So don't tell me my grief is unimportant or not as bad as others have it...it is bad. It has altered my life from the outside in, and the inside out — forever. Nothing will ever be the same again. And as I begin to pick up the millions of pieces of myself that were scattered at the moment of his death, ultimately by myself, I know the pain and grief I feel is as poignant and bitter as anyone feels, anywhere in the world. I am a refugee. I have lost my home. I need to find a voice to this pain of loss and change and grief. To try and make the silence more tolerable and make me feel less alone on this awful, awful journey.

Oh, you have spoken so clearly. Grief is a personal crisis. It is never helpful to compare losses or to create a hierarchy of loss. Saying that if you are not at the bottom of the hierarchy, maybe the pain won't be so hard. Not true. Loss is about relationship: the deeper the relationship, the deeper the loss...period. You have taught me about your relationship: a deep, intimate love that covered every part of you. Period.

Your voice roars, my friend. You are seeing truth about grief, and you are teaching me. Thank you.

As I began my drive on my adventure, six hours from home, I felt a bit numb. The car was packed, I had my snacks and water beside me, but I had always done this trip with somebody. This time there were no kids fighting in the back, no one asking to go pee, no one else to share the driving, no discussion over what music to listen to...no discussion at all. I cried. I drove. I cried. I drove. All in silence. I decided to do this trip to see if I could, if I could begin to do things again...on my own. Not just be home. Not wait for someone else to rescue me. For me to do this for me. So I put on some music, loud music, not classical... U2, Coldplay, David Bowie. And I drove differently. It still felt odd being alone in the car. Getting gas alone, running in to the bathroom with no one to keep the car running or come in with me and get something to eat, chat about other people, just share observations. Every little thing is different. But I need to realize my self now. Not as a mother, an employee, a wife, a friend... just as me. Not sure I have ever really done that. And with hours to myself in the car, those thoughts danced around my head. I know my love is with me, watching, encouraging. I hate and love him all at the same time.

I took an unfamiliar route as directed by my GPS, and all I could think was that if something happened I might never be seen again. I'd be locked in a room in a very, very old log house, and no one would ever know. I couldn't turn back, it was getting dark, and there was nowhere to turn around, so I continued on the very curvy, twisty, scary road, hoping it would come to a highway soon. My stomach started to ache. I was wishing I'd just stayed home. I was missing my big, burly husband who would protect me and figure out what to do. But there was just me. Just me. So I took a deep breath and told myself to drive carefully, put some classical music on to keep calm, and just keep driving.

Now it was getting dark. I hoped it wouldn't be much farther. Finally, a bit of a mess, and a lot of driving in circles, hair everywhere, and thin patience, I stood in front of the reception desk. At this point I was almost in tears because I knew I still had to carry the bags up by myself, go in elevators, which I didn't like, and park the car in an underground lot, which has always freaked me out. I reminded myself this was exactly why I was here. The attendant could see I was flustered and hungry. "Just park outside and go across the road and eat, come back after and deal with the bags." A good idea. So after three pints of beer and a bowl of noodles and veggies, I was ready to park the car, deal with the bags, elevators, and room keys. And I did. Maybe not well, maybe things kept falling off the cart, maybe I had the wrong key and had to keep lugging myself and my bags up and down the elevator until security took pity on me and got me the correct key, maybe I dropped all the bags on the floor, stripped off my clothes, and fell into bed. But I had done it. I was here. In this big, big, BIG room. Now what?

You have just had a huge success. Bask in that for a moment!!

The success of making the decision to step out of your own safe space of home and moving outward. Find YOU. Wow. Think about all that you just did and learned about yourself. You have courage. You have a capacity you didn't know you had. You are able to find ways to calm yourself when anxiety begins to well up. You talked to yourself and listened to your own wisdom to help you move forward.

But I'm frozen. Maybe I used up all my courage. I'm scared grief will slip back in. How do I leave the room now?

Stay in the room for a while. Stay and be still, like you used to do in your chair. Stay until you want to walk forward. Perhaps this trip was about finding out just how far you can go. Maybe that's all you need for this big first trip. You know where to get something to eat, you know where to get a drink and maybe that's all — and that's OK. Be kind to yourself. Breathe. Be still. Remember...it's OK.

Right. True. It was a big step. Maybe I'll just curl up in the bed and watch a movie. Then I'll see.

Good plan. One step at a time.

Blank Page Suggestion:
Make a list of places you'd like to visit, adventures you could do, big or small. Don't worry about the details now; it's your wish list.

163

Green Moment

My husband died of a heart attack in our backyard, under the cedar trees. A friend of mine said to me around that time, "Plant the seeds here, the seeds he has given you to grow." At the time, I didn't really know what she meant. I didn't want any seeds. I wanted him. I still want him, but I have begun to think about the seed thing more. Whether I like it or not, there is a circle of life, no beginning and no end. That is a bizarre concept to grasp for the finite brain. Especially when I stand at what clearly is an end. But my friend was saying it wasn't an end, that there were seeds to be planted and new things to grow. I made a small garden in the place he died with a bench so I could have coffee with him in the mornings, and I would sit there with him. And slowly, reluctantly, begrudgingly, I began to allow myself to contemplate those seeds, to crack them open. I started to plant some, and I am watching. They are slow to grow, require a lot of attention, and will just stop advancing if unattended. But there is a shift, a movement. I'm not sure what these seeds will produce. It is a world entirely located in the unknown, which is very unsettling. I loved the known world with my husband. But I can't just sit in this little sacred garden. And who knows, maybe they're magic seeds. Jack had magic beans that led him to worlds outside his own, full of richness and adventure. I can't think my love would give me anything but magic seeds. So I am being a little more brave each day, attending to the seeds and watching what magic is collecting in the unknown.

Your friend gave you a good idea, but it wasn't the time for you to act on it. She gave you an invitation to look at the loss differently, but you weren't ready to. And now you are — ready to try to slowly move toward a new place in your grief. Maybe you are a seed being cracked open as well. Kept out of the ground, it's safe; moving into the rich earth, it has a chance to slowly and magically grow into life. The magic seeds. Find someone to come and join you in your garden.

Oh, I would so love that.

Blank Page Suggestion:
Write about a place that could be a refuge for you, your happy place.

165

I'm learning on this unwelcome journey. In order to move beyond the confines that grief presents and wraps me in, I need to be still inside. I need to still my thoughts, emotions, ideas, memories...really everything. For a time, I need to be utterly still inside. That is where I find me. Whoever that may now be. That is a place I rarely, if ever frequented before I was pushed into this unwelcoming room with grief. The stillness is part of the new journey. When I am in that place, grief has nothing to chew on and can't fester. Grief would happily consume me, I think. In stillness, my being can generate new cells and tissues and structures that can take me beyond grief. And beyond grief I must go to survive. But first, I must be still...a certain kind of still. As with everything in grief, it is a collection of dichotomies. In order to be still inside, I must move, carefully. Yoga allows me to move carefully and just enough to steal my mind away from the shackles of grief. It allows me to mourn outside the straitjacket and reconnect with the body I inhabit. Walking is gentle movement, a kind of stillness. Walking in nature is like being wrapped in a warm, comforting blanket where I feel safe and nurtured. It allows me to be still and just listen. It takes great strength of will to move into this stillness at a time when curling into the fetal position in a corner with a box of Kleenex is all I want to do....and sometimes it is all I can do.... and sometimes it is all I should do. But when I can, I find some stillness, some reprieve, the place where I can hear again and so feel my loved one close. Grief can be a very dark place. I am allowing myself to step into the light, just to remember what it can be like, even though the light is now very, very different. Still.

You are learning! Learning what works for you, giving yourself permission to be still or curl into a corner. You are discovering what works and what helps you find your way. Nice!

Like you said, sometimes you want to do the opposite, but now you know that being still is what you need at those moments when grief wants to consume you. You aren't as afraid. You know you can find a way. Good for you!

Grief has made me brilliant at crying. Especially at this Christmassy time of year. My son wanted to get me out of the house and go shopping, not for gifts, just to get me out, I think. So I forced myself to get dressed and hang up my housecoat, take off my slippers. We went to a street in the city that was always a favourite of mine, of ours. We walked along the street, and he had his arm around my shoulders (he's very tall). There were decorations on streetlights and in store windows. It was a frosty day, and everything really was pretty. Funny how I seemed to be looking at all these things with someone else's eyes. I could see everything and register it was pretty, but there was no feeling attached. And then we walked by a window that had the exact same sweater that my sweetheart had bought for me his last Christmas, and without warning, I started to feel tears sliding down my cheeks. I had become better at silently crying; I just wailed at night or in the bush. But here, on a busy street, I couldn't move and just stood there crying silently.

My son handed me a Kleenex, hugged me, said little, and encouraged me to keep walking. "Here, let's go and get something warm to drink," he offered. And we headed for a cafe. Along the way, we passed by a sushi restaurant. "Want to come back here for lunch?" he asked. I was crying again. "What?" he asked softly.

"We loved to come here for lunch..." And that was all I could choke out. The rest of the day continued like that...being triggered by the tiniest thing would push me through that door that led into the world of tears. We got our warm drink and continued with our day, me in a kind of fog . I was exhausted when I finally got home. At least I actually slept for more than four hours that night. But I'm not sure my son will want to go out with me again too soon, or anyone else, for that matter. Maybe it's best to just stay in my housecoat.

Oh, my. You must have been exhausted! What a full day for you. Good for you for trying. Your son sounds like a caring and supportive young man. How precious that he wanted to build a moment that he hoped would help in your grief.

It may seem safer to stay in your housecoat and stay in the fog. There is a time for hibernation when we have been so deeply wounded. But remember that total insolation will not help you. Find the balance that works for you. Give yourself permission to say no and to say yes. You'll know. Begin to trust yourself.

Trust myself?

Of course, yes. Who else?

Turquoise Moments

Time becomes an odd concept when tangled with grief. As grief begins to ebb and flow, rather than gripping you breathless in its clutches, time is distorted as well. Some days and moments seem interminably long, lifetimes in fact. I can get stuck in a thought or feeling that pulls me into a fog where I wait for the next breath. But then there are those glimpses through, glimpses between those long breaths, like a gust of wind that rattles through the trees and is quickly gone. A force moving through me and around me. Urging me to move, forward, move, just move.

Today I will get in my car and drive for eight hours to an adventure. I feel driven to move into that breath, not just watch it move by me. I need to step into myself somehow. Not a needy self, not a self looking for my love in another, but truly that authentic self I can feel tapping at the window, waiting to emerge. I'm listening and watching. But I'm taking my own breath and splitting time down the middle today. All on my own.

This is a big and new step for you to venture so far away from home. Good for you!

You have learned that time and being kind to yourself allows for the ebb and flow of grief. It's something you will keep learning about, and that is OK.

Remember...it's OK!

I'm beginning to see that now. That makes me smile.

Grief is fond of ill-fitting boots. "Pull yourself up by the bootstraps." I've heard people say that to those feeling down or blue or lost. Hmmm. Never sure what that really meant, but it always sounded so harsh. I was curious about the statement, so I sat with it for a while, trying to make some sense of the whole thing. And after reflection, pulling yourself up by the bootstraps might not be a bad idea, but saying it that way should really have the boot tossed at your head. If grief is like a pair of boots, then it is like walking around with them unlaced, not quite on your heel, just your toe slipped inside but the rest just flopping around. And flopping around in a boot isn't good for your foot, or your hips, or your back. It means you are always off balance, always ready to fall over, again. Pulling up those bootstraps means pulling the boot on, heel inside, laces tied up, secure, balanced. When the boot is on properly, there isn't room for grief; there isn't room for flopping around and losing your balance. You walk straight and tall, your step is firm and confident and you know you will get to the end of the road safely.

So I'm trying to pull up my bootstraps, or to say it more gently, find a way to slip into my boots all the way and lace them up snugly. It might be time to start walking along the path balanced and tall, in good-fitting footwear.

There was a time when your boots just didn't fit. Couldn't fit. Telling someone to pull themselves up by the bootstraps is harsh in early grief; in fact, like the original saying, it's actually impossible. Bootstrapping refers to a self-starting process that happens without external input. But the original was actually a tongue-in-cheek kind of saying. The term appears to have originated in early nineteenth century United States (particularly in the phrase "pull oneself over a fence by one's bootstraps") to mean an absurdly impossible action. You are becoming self-starting...bootstrapping. Woo-hoo.

But in the early days of grief, in the fog with no energy, it's kind of absurd, isn't it? The things people say.

Yeah — that's for sure!

Grief pauses inside entrances to our dreams. When sleep finally washed over me last night, there he was standing before me. We walked together, he kissed me, and I could feel it and taste it. I could hear myself say I loved him and feel his warmth soak into my cells, my skin. He caressed my cheek like only he could do, and we laughed at silly things. My body craved him, ached for him. It felt so full, so real. I knew he was with me. The light of morning pushed itself through the window, and I moved into wakefulness only to be forced back to the reality that his place was still empty. That his absence in my wakeful state was still oh so very real. My heart beat faster, my cheeks flushed in pain, my stomach lurched. It was true: he was gone. But he had been there in my dream, which felt so real. Do I find him in that moment between — like waking into mists and feeling their wisps of wetness on my face, reaching to grasp them as they melt away? But the mists are there, quietly hovering, stretching. I think I'll just close my eyes and see if I can quickly catch him again.

It is beautiful to see how your dreams have changed. Now these precious dreams full of love and intimacy. Yes, close your eyes and be with him whenever you can.

Oh, I will. And the thought makes me smile.

Blank Page Suggestion:
Write about one of your dreams. Recount it.

177

When he first died, I would not walk through the doorway that led to the boxes of Christmas lights and decorations. There were feelings and faces and smells and sounds in those boxes that I knew would kill me, take too much out of my physical being to survive. So the boxes and the door stayed in shadow. One year later, I still will not walk through that door. I've discovered that memories are not just imaginings of the mind. They are captured events held in time and space forever. They hold substance and come wrapped in all the five senses. They enter into us through our pores and cells, not just as pictures in our mind. They pull on blood pressure, digestion, headaches, muscle fatigue, and distort our current reality. Memories are complicated, integral things not to be taken lightly. So I knew I was not ready, may never be ready, to open those boxes. But I also knew that I didn't want my house to remain static forever. I love colour and light, so I created something new. I didn't go and get a tree with an axe, like we used to do...I bought an artificial tree, lights we had never used before in a totally different colour, and only silver and white baubles of different sizes for the tree. Nothing else. Blue lights, silver baubles, and the silver tie that had bound the bauble box. And I decorated the tree. My son, a young man now who comes to visit, sat on the floor, putting the hooks on the baubles, handing them to me, directing me to empty spots on the tree. It was awkward at first, but we found a rhythm. We found a Christmas moment together. My new silver and blue Christmas memory. It looked like an icicle, like a winter moment in my living room. It doesn't have the warmth and brilliance of the tree my husband and I decorated; it is different. But it brings a special energy to the house. I find a half smile when I plug in the lights and all the silver baubles sparkle. My husband is there in a twinkle, and so is my son. It's a beginning.

You created something new, and it was beautiful and meaningful. Good for you! You knew you were ready and listened to your heart and brought colour and energy back into a season that had been dreaded. You also knew that the tree and ornaments you shared with your love were not going to be part of this year's story. They may never be. And that is OK.

Your tree is beautiful and reflects the colour and beauty that is coming back to you. So lovely.

Imagine sitting together and feeling the healing movement of grief.

I will. Thanks.

When my husband died, our dog left the building, heart and soul. He'd hide anytime I cried. The happy, friendly Shephard now growled if men walked in the house and would bare his teeth if they tried to touch him. He would only eat if I was in the room, and the animal that never even chewed a shoe as a puppy now chewed through door frames if I left the house. He was deeply injured by the loss of his alpha dog and friend. And as I watched him, I knew that if I could, I would act the same. As time passed, I watched pieces of his confidence return, but he was always leery of men. And then last night, he came with me to dinner at some friends (I do that more often now), and the man of the house reached out, and my dog went to him. Not only went to him, played with him, lay beside him at dinner, kissed him. My dog felt a comfort with a man he had not felt since his master had died. And as I watched all this unfold, my heart opened to these possibilities for healing. There is no hidden agenda with an animal, no pretense and pretending...just raw, real response and pain. And tonight he crossed a bridge and collected a few more pieces of himself. We were healing together. Watching his pain was a reflection of my own, but he owned his better, I think. Watch your animals, comfort them, understand them, and by doing so, understand your own journey a little bit better.

What a precious moment. The animals in our life know when a big change has happened and when big emotions are present. It sounds like your dog was very connected to your love. Just like you were. You allowed your dog to go at his pace, you were kind to him; you couldn't take his pain away but you found ways to comfort him. And he found his way. Yes, I think this will help you understand your own journey a bit better. And how to be that kind and good to yourself.

Blank Page Suggestion:
If you have an animal, tell me what you remember about how they suffered the loss of their master.

I have stepped back from the gaping, original black hole of grief, only to find myself at yet another precipice. how to re-enter the world. How do I re-enter a world that has remained relatively static, while I have been to hell and back, changed. People say words, but often it is just lips moving and not from a deeper place. But now I am coming from a deeper place. A place that knows work is important, but relationships are really all we have. A place that says we don't have a luxury to wait, because things are taken at a moment's notice. And without walking the journey, others think that means I am needy or hasty. Maybe that is true, but I realize I do need others, like never before. To complete me? No. I can only complete myself. Grief has taught me that. But I need others for different things: to reflect me, to mark my journey, to exchange ideas and feelings, to share skin on skin. That leaves me in grief again. In a game of guessing. And am I hasty? Eager to not waste moments, eager to connect with life, eager to engage in and outside myself that only happens with others? Yes, then I am hasty. Maybe I don't fit any more. With anyone. Has grief and loss and death made me an orphan forever?

No, you are not an orphan. You have been adopted into a new family with a new identity.

What you have learned about yourself has changed how you want to live and how you want to be in relationships. There can even be more grief as you realize some of the people that you were close to aren't able to understand the new you, and you will begin to feel some distance. Or you may find there are some who would like to get to know that new you but are scared and find it difficult to go into deeper emotions. And then there will be some new friends that you have made along your grief journey, safe people who want to have those deeper conversations. Now that you know what you know, you can't go back. Yes, you are eager and that is beautiful. Remember when you couldn't imagine ever wanting to connect with people again for fear of losing them? And here you are, ready. And well equipped to know who is safe and in your corner. Welcome to your new world.

Turquoise Moment

Today looks fresh
it's cool and clear
trees stand tall
no wind to bend or sway.
Quiet, strong.
But I don't feel so tall today
not so cool or clear
Not so strong.
You're not here
and I miss you.
I miss you.
I still miss you.

I know.

What is it to miss someone? Maybe it's wanting that empty space to be filled, to have them back to fill it. But then my mind takes over. I begin to remember him. I can just live in my mind's imagination of him being back and filling that spot. Problem is, when I do that, I'm not in the moment that I'm in. And things pass me by. But what if I don't imagine him any more? What if I just live in my current moments and even come to enjoy them without him? Am I betraying him? Will I forget him?

No, you won't forget him.

As you have begun to move forward, there comes with that movement the natural fear of forgetting. It can feel like the only way not to forget him is to keep him present in your thoughts at all times — as current and real as possible. But as you have also seen, it becomes hard to do that when new experiences come. The work you have been doing in grief has anchored him in your heart and in your body — all your senses will remember, your memories will remember, your dreams will remember...and you will remember. And you won't have to be frantic to keep his memory fresh; he is part of the fabric of your life. And you won't forget him.

I won't forget him, I won't. OK.

Turquoise Moment

I retreat
into myself
quiet, musing, watching
trying to find my new rhythm
with self
with others
looking for patience
listening for clues
readjusting pieces
allowing my world to expand
allowing myself
to expand
into
learning
on how to walk this place
alone
and yet beside others
as they carry their own
perspectives
so different from my own.

I'm sitting with a tea, comforted by these beautiful words.
    Thank you.

Grief. It is like diving into an ocean with no tank, finding the light getting thinner, the air almost gone, and then my hand reaches out and folds around a small object. I hold it tightly as I float to the surface, and when I open my hand, the oyster presents its pearl. Even the pearl was created from grains of sand caught, grieving, trapped, and disturbing to each other.

That moment when I float to the surface and take that long deep breath, that energy of life, is the moment I truly began to choose life. And as I put myself back together, my priorities and views have changed. Bills still need to be paid, mortgages paid, jobs attended to, but they are peripheral. Suddenly, culturally held views are irrelevant, fear is replaced by opportunities, and people I stand beside are chosen through deep movings of the heart, nothing else. And by choosing life, I choose to be touched by raindrops on my skin, be caught in the stillness of a forest, be drawn into the abandon of airborne hawks. All because of one breath.

I love that image. I remember when you asked me if you would be able to breathe because the blanket of grief was so thick and heavy on you. Remember that? And here is a new experience of breath… life-giving, transforming, and full. Take a deep breath and be aware of how far you have come and where you are now in your journey. Like the grain of sand, you are also being changed.

That makes me smile.

Society doesn't like dirty stuff, so it gives a really, really small window of time to grieve. You know, just get over it so we can talk about wallpaper and new couches and recipes. So we all walk around invisible, holding ourselves together...for what? Well, so we can get and keep a job, I guess. Socialize, you know, acceptably. Watch the Super Bowl together. Big laughter, lots of alcohol, bawdy jokes, carefree. Anything less is well, really, a wet blanket, and no one wants to be a wet blanket, now do we? I think we need more wet blankets. They put out fires that will otherwise consume us and leave us in ashes. They are cooling on a hot day and allow for clear-headed thinking. What's wrong with the wet blanket? And how dare anyone tell me that what I'm sad about isn't something I should be sad about. Or to tell me I should stop being sad about it. Forget that. Disenfranchised grief. Sounds like a food chain gone bad. Sounds like a fancy word to cover up the fact that we live amongst thieves who rob us of wholeness. And we let them do it. I think we need to start the Wet Blanket Club and throw it wholeheartedly on disenfranchised grief.

Sadly, you have learned how grief-avoidant our society is. It is not a soft place for grieving and mourning people. You have seen how unrealistic expectations are; how they don't match the reality or the journey with loss. Grief is seen as something to be avoided. You have also seen how moving into your grief actually opened you up to see with new eyes and brought clear-headed thinking. There is a new kind of understanding of grief, of life, of yourself, of others that only your journey with grief could bring you.

The Wet Blanket Club — I think you have something there!

Thanks.

Pale Blue
Moments

My sweetheart was wonderful at buying me gifts. He never left it to the last minute. He would always tell me the story of the gift adventure after I had opened it, eyes wide with joy. The story was as wonderful as the gift. He would choose special things. Things that said he watched me. Listened to me. Loved me. He had beautiful hands, but he was a big guy, so his hands were big too. I always marvelled at how delicately and intricately he would wrap my gifts. Little tied ribbons, perfectly folded edges, tiny pieces of tape. Gifts I wrapped always looked like the dog had wrapped them. But his were almost too beautiful to open. I would sit with this gorgeous little box on my lap, admiring the wrapping. "Well, aren't you going to open it?" he would ask, eager to see my reaction. It wouldn't have mattered what was in the box, really; the effort and love wrapped all around it was always gift enough. One year, he had come across an artisan who made her own fine silver jewellery, and he asked her to make me a special pair of earrings in the shape of a horse and a small bracelet to match. He knew how special horses were to me. He had helped her design them. They were exquisite. The story of their creation and how excited he was to give them to me burst my heart with love for this gentle, wonderful man who loved me so dearly. I had never really known love before him. When I opened the little box (so very carefully so I could put the wrapping back on the empty box, or get him to), I couldn't believe the beauty of the contents. I rushed over, hopped into his lap, and kissed that wonderful man, my husband. He was so wonderful to kiss. Such a mouth made for kissing. Especially birthday kisses. "Thank you my darling, they are just beautiful. I will treasure them always." And he held me close, like only he could do.

I am watching your face as you share this beautiful memory. Your eyes are sparkling, your voice is rich, your words are full of descriptions, your energy is vibrant and alive. Now this memory is a treasure. There was a time when memories only brought pain. Yes, even this one still brings feelings of loss, but look at how you can hold the happy and the sad together now. The grief work you have done now allows you to savour the sweet pleasure of this memory. How precious.

Thank you for telling me. I feel uplifted.

Blank Page Suggestion:
Draw a birthday cake. How many candles would there be? Make a
wish for your love...and yourself.

197

Years can pass. You come to accept the different life devoid of your love. You go to work, socialize, engage in healthy activities, laugh, travel. You are in the world again and not the tiny black box of pain and no possibilities. Right.

And then a few days bounce into each other; you don't feel well but still engage in work and with others, issues arise that are not in line with your thinking, things begin affecting you, and the spiral begins. All of a sudden, in the middle of the angst around you, an image of your lost love pops in front of your eyes, and that's it, you're gone. Tears rolling down your face, sobs shaking your body. At that moment it doesn't matter if you are standing on the top of a ski hill, at the edge of an ocean, on a busy downtown street corner, just been handed a winning lottery ticket, in an elevator, in your bedroom...it doesn't matter. You are now lost in grief once again. Fuck.

It's all-consuming, as grief is. You want to go back. You want things to be the way they were. Everything swirls around you and time just pauses. The difference from before is that there is a tiny window on the edge of your mind that you are aware of. And you know that this time you will not be lost in the dark hole, trapped in the black box for months and months and months. You know there is a window out and that the grief will not consume you this time.

But in that moment, oh God, how you miss your love and want them back. For comfort, for advice, for love, for them.

And then you take a deep breath, open the window, and carry on.

Yes. The depth of your pain, even in these months and years later, reminds you of the depth of your love and your loss. You remember. You will always remember. Your love is part of your world, plain and simple. You remember and remembering brings pain and brings an intimacy of just you and your love. Such a bittersweet residual impact of deep loss.

But those moments...oh, those moments. They are the placard of the depth of your love; the depth of your loss; the depth of your hard work to find your way in your grief. Bravo!

Yesterday, I went shopping in the afternoon with my son. Out of the blue, I asked him if there was a music store around. When we went in, a name popped into my head out of nowhere — Coldplay. OK, I said, do they have a new album. Apparently they did...so we bought it. And when I listened to the last song, "Up and Up," I knew that the album was put into my head by my love. That song is my inspiration now...it is the magic I was hoping for...it allows me to reach outside my grief. To reach up and up. Coldplay got it. They really got it.

When I sang along with the song that I will pull things together, which I desperately need to do, I suddenly understood what that really meant. I saw pieces of myself all over the floor, in various shapes and sizes. And I started to sweep them together. And this year, I will begin to pull myself together. Begin. The pieces will never fit together the same way, never. But they will fit together. And now I am putting them together one by one. Each day I find a piece that wants to fit somewhere. I don't know how long it will take, where it will lead, or what I will look like at the end. It will be a different me. But I'm curious.

And I won't give up. My darling would never want me to just be a puddle on the floor, on the floor forever. I have to honour him and myself...so I'm pulling myself together, to flow and go...up...and...up.

You are honouring your love. :)

And myself at the same time.

Indeed.

Blank Page Suggestion:
What are some songs that inspire you? Make a new playlist for yourself.

201

Boxing Day wasn't always just sales that lasted one or two weeks with up to 30% off. Boxing Day originally was the day after Christmas when boxes that had held precious gifts and were strewn about the living room now had a day to be folded up into their flat form and taken to the garbage or burn pile. It was the day to deal with boxes. Simple. Today, as I deal with boxes and wrinkled, crinkled wrapping paper, I realized that my grief needs a Boxing Day. It needs to be flattened and folded and put into the garbage or burn pile. Just like the boxes, it takes up a lot of space and makes it difficult to move around, get back to regular things. The tricky thing with grief is it acts like a jack-in-the-box and pops up out of nowhere to scare me. But I will try to box it, at least some of it anyway. And the part that keeps popping up, that still brings tears to my eyes and aches in my heart, well, I'll just have to deal with that while I push little Jack back down into his box for the next time. Maybe soon Jack will cease to work at all, and all the boxes of grief will finally and permanently be boxed. Today, I'll just box as many as I can.

Boxing grief — I like that picture. Sometimes Jack will jump out with a grief moment for you, and at other times you will take a box down from the shelf and open it yourself and hold what you find inside. You are now more able to manage the mess that grief created. You are creating order in your life again — one box at a time.

"I'll do right by you." I remember hearing that song line in my head very soon after his death. And as I am more settled, I hear my love more. I hear that line more too. There are questions I have about where I need to live, what I should do, who to choose, how to be. I choose different clothes to wear these days. Actually, I'd like to throw all my clothes out and start fresh. There are no rules any more. Thing is, I do have to be cautious, thoughtful about next moves. So I'm putting things out there and waiting to see what comes back. I feel more and more centered, and then I slip and feel anxious. But I gather myself more quickly now, and my mind goes around and around. That's how I'm feeling. But the thing about no rules really does feel true. There is a letting go that happens, and that is a really hard door to step through. But that door has interesting vibes. So I had to stay behind, and I still have a physical body that is talking very loudly these days. For many, many days after my other half died, I lived between that world and mine, not in my body but not able to be here, not recognize it. Now I have slipped into my body more, the physical world around me, and can touch this other world as I need to, feel it around me. It's the better balance. No rules. I like that. Really in the world, but not of the world. I finally get that. Maybe it's time to figure out what this physical world really has to offer. I'm here...might as well. Could be fun. And my sweetheart seems to smile when I think like that. Could be fun. I know now my love is watching. 'I'll do right by you', he sings.

As you are talking I picture a fledgling trying out its wings. There was a time when the fledgling needed the rules — stay in the nest! Learn what you can and can't trust! You learned what and who helps you in life; you learned about your own courage; you learned that limits were especially important, because you were so fragile. And now you are beginning to spread those wings. And maybe leaving the safety of the little nest you built is OK and even could be fun.

The smile of your sweetheart — I have seen how precious a thought that is to you. His presence, smile, and touch gave you a life of intimacy. When you lost him, you also lost the deep intimacy that you two shared...another layer of loss.

Yes. It's hard to say this, not sure why, but my body misses him. We had great sex together. Now what do I do? I don't know how I would ever trust anyone like that again. But I am still in this physical body, and it is talking very loudly these days. Maybe because it had no voice at all for so long. I don't know. But it is awake now. What on earth do I do? Help!

Every part of you is awakening. And like all the other parts of you, you will find what works for your physical body. Will it be pampering it with a massage? Finding personal ways to feel the intimacy again? Will it be pouring your energy into physical activity? Are you ready to look into meeting someone else? You are listening to the voice of your body again. Listen. There is no wrong answer. Remember how you said all the rules have changed? Trust yourself.

I used to be terrified of the dark. If there wasn't a night light on, I would break into a sweat just to get up and go to the bathroom. I'm not really sure what I was afraid of, but the darkness held some unseen lurking terror. In early morning hours, still dark in northern Ontario winters, I would stand at my front door and count down, then run to my car, which stood in the pitch dark. My love changed all that. Suddenly, if the night light was out or the power went off, he would find my hand, give it a squeeze, and everything would be OK. He had that kind of astounding effect on me. Things just settled, and terror lurking evaporated. Even if he didn't have to get up early to go to work, up he would get, slip into his robe, step into his winter boots, and go outside to clean my car off and stand there until I was safely in. He'd kiss me and tell me to drive safely. I'd blow a kiss as I drove off, knowing my love would soon be back snuggled in our warm bed. Off I would go, happy as a little clam. Then he died and darkness was everywhere, even in the middle of the day. But somehow, I wasn't afraid any more. My love is with me, and that is a comfort. In many ways losing him was the scariest thing I could ever experience. Nothing else can really top that. I still don't like the dark much, but my love used to say that there was a peace in the nothingness of darkness. So I am trying to see that and maybe find him there, waiting for me, hand held out.

Oh, what a memory.

I'm catching my breath at the beauty of these words.

Remember when memories like this would bring you such emptiness and pain?

This beautiful memory has brought you comfort this time, and more than that, it has given you courage and a sense that he is with you forever.

Yes, I do remember, and it is becoming OK. You were right. The journey changes. How did you know? And how did you know not to tell me sooner?

Think back over all our conversations; you took the lead, letting me know when you were ready to see things in a new way. Now you know.

Yes, I'm starting to. Thanks.

I moved two years after he died. I just couldn't stay in the same house any more; it was thick with us. And there was no us. So I moved. I've been here for almost three years now, and I realized, today, I haven't been here at all until now. I've been a ghost in my body, in my house, going through the motions. Cleaning, working, smiling, talking to people. I brought everything with me when I moved, even though the new place was half the size of the other. Yes, it was cramped. Cluttered, and I hate that. But I needed his desk, his books, his bike, his chair, and on and on and on. And then two weeks ago I got up in the morning and decided right there on the spot, I didn't want this clutter any more. I didn't need these things. They were just that, things. Not him. And so I started to sell furniture, get rid of bags of clothes, bags of items that I was hanging on to, like somehow it would be like a trail of breadcrumbs and he'd find his way back to me. But that morning, I knew he wouldn't. And I knew it was my turn. My house feels lighter. It's becoming mine. And finally, I'm OK with that. I don't feel guilty any more for not having died too. Do I still miss him? Oh, yes. Terribly. Do I sometimes still want to go out back and grab on to a tree and scream...sometimes. Sometimes it still feels like yesterday when he left, and yet it doesn't. Lines are blurred and yet crystal clear. Does this make any sense at all?

Indeed, it does make sense. Part of the work of grief is to find your "new" identity — an identity that now aligns with the reality of your loss. You have to do it at your own pace. Remember your friends that urged you to purge? They had the right idea, but they did not understand it could only be when you were ready. You can be proud of yourself. You listened to yourself and you were kind to YOU in these big changes.

Thank you, it feels good to be so understood.

Maybe the story of Sleeping Beauty is really about a person who lost their love and was in the depths of grief. It is like that in many ways, the grief experienced from the loss of a loved one. You slip into a long, long sleep, where things that you do and say are dreamlike, ephemeral. The actual sense of touch and feeling isn't present in that sleep state. When you sleep or nap, the sense of sound will be the first thing to rouse you from your slumber. But when you are in a grief-sleep, your physical body and its many senses slowly begin to stir, awaken. It is like experiencing splinters of light quickening through your veins at the unexpected touch of another, or witnessing a beautiful sunset and actually absorbing that glow. Suddenly, you are touched. You feel it. It is a memory, but you feel it and it is different, keener, because you are different. It is finding a spontaneous laughter burst upon you from a tiny unsuspecting moment: a blue jay tossing seeds helter-skelter from the feeder, the way a dog is head over heels for a treat, a hug from a friend. And it is odd, because you notice it. You never would have before because it was common, but you notice it now because you are waking from that long, deep, and often nightmarish sleep.

Sleeping Beauty was wakened by the kiss of a prince who braved the brambles to reach her bedside. It certainly could be an amorous kiss that begins a warmth in your veins, so long cold and afraid. But it could also be the kiss of a snowflake as it settles on your cheek, and you softly wipe it away as it begins to melt, feeling the sensation and finding yourself lingering in that moment. Or sun on your skin tingling each cell, the taste of a rich wine on your tongue reawakening your senses.

This awakening can't be rushed. I have been asleep a long time. I need to be gentle and slow as muscles take time to move, breath comes lightly, the light will be bright in my eyes. But I am waking. I may be groggy and need time to fully collect myself. And then I will tend to that very overgrown garden inside my walls.

I'm enjoying the discoveries you're making. I'm just sitting in the middle of this moment and taking it in fully.

I think grief calls us up. Challenges us to step out of our routines. Moves us out of our comfort zone. Shows us that there is more than what we see with our eyes. Grief makes us feel and feel and feel, often to the point of exhaustion. But I have become more aware. I am more aware of thoughts that pop into my head, because now I wonder where they come from. As I was going about my morning routine of feeding the dogs, there was no radio on, the room was quiet, and I was slowly moving around. As I put the dog's bowl down, phrases moved around in my head. I stood up and paid attention, listening carefully to what the words actually were saying. It was a song I knew by Richard Marx, an eighties classic, "Right Here Waiting."

I listened as the words circled around and around in my head. I just knew it was my husband talking to me, communicating through lyrics, telling me he is still close by. I went to my computer and searched the first words of the song, and there it was. I read all the lyrics. I started to weep and closed my eyes. My love was hurting too, he saw my pain and could do nothing, but he was there, right beside me. I could feel him all around me. The words from the song were his words. I will have to begin to listen more carefully to the voices in my head, because now I knew they weren't just mine. In this tiny moment, grief had opened a door that otherwise I would never have known existed.

Oh, the curious, strange, wonderful, hard gifts of grief and loss. You are now able to be open to them. A song isn't just a song when it holds the heart of your love. And you will experience more and more moments like this. Intimate moments that speak the language of your heart, the language of your love. Yes, tears may flow in the middle of the sweet gift. It's that happy/sad thing that expands us to be able to hold so much more as we have journeyed with loss. Thanks for sharing the words of this song. I had never noticed them before. A new gift for me too.

That makes me very happy.

I watched a romance movie for the first time in a long time. By myself. At the romance part, my reaction was not what I was expecting. I didn't feel sad or want to turn it off because I didn't have that any more. I felt glad that they had that special feeling. And then I imagined it was me and my honey. It was all rather disconnected, but there was gratitude for what I had, what we experienced, rather than sadness at not having it, him, any more. It surprised me. I watched the whole movie. I'm not sure it was a popcorn kind of movie moment, but it was soulful and I felt warm and content when it was over. I had something special. I really did.

I love how you can see when something like this happens — when you are surprised by the changes in your journey. Now you can take in something that at the beginning was impossible to tolerate. And not only can you take it in, you can enjoy it, and even connect your own romance story with feelings of gratitude. What a special surprise.

Yes it was, it really was.

Blank Page Suggestion:
Create a list of your favourite movies. Invite some friends over for movie night.

I am coming to find that my soul, my spirit, welcomes silence. The fullness of quiet. Like the solid, all-encompassing silence of swimming underwater. And it is in this quiet, serene silence that the spirit sings. It is here that I find my love again. Moments of silence in an oh-so-busy and noisy world. I welcome the hush of noiselessness.

I'm listening with you.

Mmmm. Yes.

I think grief is like sunstroke. If you get it once, you always have a proclivity to getting it again. Once you've been touched by death, you are never the same again. It's like you cross over a line into this dark zone. A space you would never, ever choose. But you did step over. You survived but have the scars to prove it. And some of those scars aren't quite healed and maybe never will be. So you have trouble with things now, trouble you didn't have before. Like when you have to leave a person or a place, just to say goodbye as you go on to something else, but it seems to take on a larger meaning. A mini death, almost. And so transitions of any kind require a lot of self-will to see you through to the other side. You hold your breath a little better, because that helps. But grief has touched you, and every other thing in your life has become slightly raw and exposed. You can't change that you got sunstroke, just like you can't change that someone died. All you can be now is aware and use tools to get through the transitions, opening the old scars as little as possible.

So true. There are these life lessons that we could never know without having grieved. Knowing that transitions of any kind will have grief attached to them is a huge gift. The tools you are using to find your way through the loss of your loved one will be the tools you can use in other changes you experience.

You have been changed. You have been to one of the hardest places you ever could have imagined. You survived. And not just survived but have given the grief journey a place in your being that now informs you about life and living.

The scars, the battle wounds, are constant reminders of your courage and your hard work through grief. Treat them gently, because they're loaded with meaning.

Thank you. Thank you for helping me walk this path of grief. I am eternally grateful. I couldn't have done it without you.

Thank you for trusting me to walk this path of grief with you. We have both been changed. What a sweet gift grief has given us.

Dedicated to a lost loved one

Light
(A song by musician Niina Rosa, gifted to *Remember, It's OK*)

Saw your spirit float away
Nothing's ever gonna be the same
I don't know how to
Communicate
Communicate

I think we got it all wrong
Had our eyes closed all along
But that's why we gotta have faith

Don't be scared
Don't let 'em keep you blind
Just follow the light
Just follow the light

Thought I lost something
Thought I had nothing
Then I realized it's all inside
No one can take this away
No one can take this from you

For a while I was runnin'
Scared of myself yeah
For a while I was hopin'
Someone would tell me what to do

I think we got it all wrong
Had our eyes closed all along
But that's why we gotta have faith

Don't be scared
Don't let 'em keep you blind
Just follow the light
Just follow the light

Blank Pages for Your Story

Blank Pages for Your Story

Blank Pages for Your Story

Blank Pages for Your Story

Blank Pages for Your Story

ABOUT THE AUTHORS

Author of *Primrose Street*, **Marina L. Reed** (honB.A., M.A., B.Ed.) has worked as a researcher and writer for CBC Television, and has lived and worked in countries around the world as an author, educator, journalist and artist. Her experiences are brought to life through her fiction and non-fiction writing. She is a great lover of nature, of animals, and the empowerment of individuals. Follow her at Marinalreed.com.

Founder of Griefwalk, **Marian Grace Boyd** (B.R.E., B.A.Psych, M.A. Counselling Psych.) has 30+ years experience as a psychotherapist, adoption practitioner, and grief counsellor. She brings her formal training and experiences of grief together in order to cocreate *Remember, It's OK*. Marian is passionate about helping people find peace. Follow her on www.instagram.com/rememberitisok.

Disclaimer

This book is designed to provide information and motivation to our readers. The authors are not obliged or committed to provide any type of psychological, legal, or other professional advice on a personal basis. The authors are not liable for any physical, psychological, emotional, or financial damages including but not limited to special, incidental, consequential, or other damages as a result of reading this book. The reader is responsible for his or her own choices, actions, and results.

TESTIMONIALS

All I can say is WOW! This book is amazing! I love the format, the way the feelings of grief, loss, and mourning are highlighted. The interactive aspect and the help and support worked so well. And it allowed for moments where you can think, process on your own, and make your own personal notes. As I read the book, each page captured so many of the feelings I went through after my wife passed away. It brought tears to my eyes remembering. The various colours of each section emphasize that there is a light at the end of the darkness, and the light gets bigger as time goes by. Thank you so much.

Mark Schneider

I wish I'd had this book sooner after my love died. I didn't feel I had anyone I could talk to and that no one understood me. She was my everything. I wasn't getting good advice from anyone and I was scared to say anything. I was so isolated. You made me feel that what I was feeling was OK. I wasn't going crazy. And you gave me good things to do, to think, to feel to help me through. I feel less alone having your book. And you're right, I go back and forth through the colours as I feel that day. Thank you so much.

Sarah Milton

I have had many losses, but nothing could have prepared me for the sudden loss of my husband of twenty-four years. I found myself widowed at the age of forty-six and I felt out of place with nowhere to turn. Opening the pages of Remember, It's OK was like sitting down with an old friend. Reading the moments was very visceral, they made me feel as though I was heard and understood. Those were my words, my feelings! I related to it instantly and because of that, it immediately earned my trust. I felt the safety of it wrap around me. This book is like no other grief book I have read. I believe it's not something you just read. I experienced it. It is a constant caring companion. Something I know will grow with me throughout my journey. It honours my grief by giving me ideas on ways to express and work through my loss. There is something so powerful about the visual relation to colours that makes this book so unique. It evokes emotion and I felt a progression as I moved through the colours. Almost like a rainbow I began to feel hopeful that something beautiful can grow out of the pain and loss. I wish I had had this book earlier in my journey. The blank pages where it offers and encourages you to draw, create and put self care to paper are very healing. I know it will be a book I will gift often to others. Its very title kept subliminally reminding me it's OK, when I didn't even know I needed to keep hearing that. People in mourning so need to keep hearing that! Thank you to the authors for bringing this gentle, healing hug of a book to the world. It is so needed!

Rachel Verkerke

This book had an impact on me.

As I read through the collection of moments in this book, I felt like someone was candidly describing part of my own life to me, and I could see things I hadn't noticed before. Remember things I thought I'd forgotten. Like how grief has the power to utterly shake your world and entire being so you end up losing touch with who you are. Some Moments read like a page out of my own diary, and put together they perfectly illustrate something I have experienced to be ever-present in my own grief: disjointedness, confusion, unpredictability. There is no short cut through grief, but there is a way. This book can be a window you can look through and see light.

If you are at the place where grief is all there is, this book can help you. I remember when it felt like grief was all there was; there was no hope, things felt like they would never change. I believe this book can be a hope-holder for you, something to turn to, and to help you remember it's OK.

If you experienced grief a while ago, this book will remind you how light slowly reentered your life. It will help you look back at yourself with kindness and see victory instead of inadequacy. It may soften some things, and still offer healing even if you're looking back through that window of grief, which is always slightly open.

And if you're someone trying to help someone who is grieving, a friend or loved one, this book can act as a guide for you, help you understand how that person is feeling and thinking, encourage you to simply be there.

I truly believe this book will be a gem for many different people on this grief journey.

Karen Fisher

NEXT CHAPTER PRESS

We create books that help people through life's transitions.

We all face changes, transitions, and life-altering experiences during the story of our life. From milestones to tragedies, some chapters are joyful and exciting, while others are sad and challenging.

If you are turning a page in your life, we hope our books will be a source of comfort, strength and inspiration. Written by people who have been through what you're experiencing or have helped others along a similar path, our books will help you move forward with experiences shared, lessons learned, and wisdom gained.

Everyone's story is written with many chapters, and we hope our books accompany you during this next stage of your life and help make it as meaningful as possible.

An Imprint of Blue Moon Publishers